OXFORD
Primary
Maths
Dictionary

OXFORD
Primary
Maths
Dictionary

Compiled by
Peter Patilla

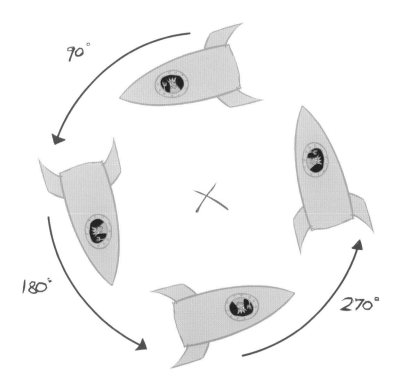

OXFORD
UNIVERSITY PRESS

OXFORD
UNIVERSITY PRESS

Great Clarendon Street, Oxford OX2 6DP

Oxford University Press is a department of the University of Oxford.
It furthers the University's objective of excellence in research, scholarship,
and education by publishing worldwide in

Oxford New York

Auckland Cape Town Dar es Salaam Hong Kong Karachi
Kuala Lumpur Madrid Melbourne Mexico CIty Nairobi New Delhi
Shanghai Taipei Toronto

With offices in

Argentina Austria Brazil Chile Czech Republic France
Greece Guatemala Hungary Italy Japan Poland Portugal Singapore
South Korea Switzerland Thailand Turkey Ukraine Vietnam

British Library Cataloguing in Publication Data available

ISBN 13-9780199109319

ISBN 0-19-910929-X Hardback
ISBN 0-19-910931-1 Paperback

5 7 9 10 8 6

Typeset in Cafeteria, Joanna and Lucida
by Macwiz
Printed in Singapore by KHL Printing Co Pte Ltd

Artists: Steve May, Colin Mier, Mark Ruffle, John Walker

Contents

Introduction

The Oxford Primary Maths Dictionary contains over 600 words in alphabetical order, each with an easy-to-understand meaning. It is an ideal way to build children's specific subject vocabulary.

The words in the Oxford Primary Maths Dictionary are drawn from the words used in primary school mathematics teaching, along with maths words that are in common everyday use. Where a word has several meanings, all of them are given.

Explanatory pictures and diagrams help make the meanings of entries clear. Captions with the word highlighted in red give further information.

The main features of the A to Z pages are:

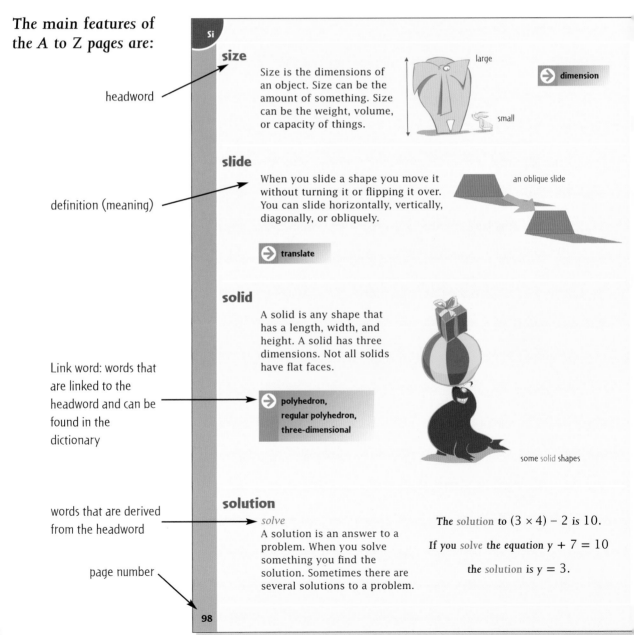

headword

definition (meaning)

Link word: words that are linked to the headword and can be found in the dictionary

words that are derived from the headword

page number

Si

size

Size is the dimensions of an object. Size can be the amount of something. Size can be the weight, volume, or capacity of things.

large

small

→ dimension

slide

When you slide a shape you move it without turning it or flipping it over. You can slide horizontally, vertically, diagonally, or obliquely.

an oblique slide

→ translate

solid

A solid is any shape that has a length, width, and height. A solid has three dimensions. Not all solids have flat faces.

→ polyhedron,
regular polyhedron,
three-dimensional

some solid shapes

solution

solve
A solution is an answer to a problem. When you solve something you find the solution. Sometimes there are several solutions to a problem.

The solution to $(3 \times 4) - 2$ is 10.

If you solve the equation $y + 7 = 10$

the solution is $y = 3$.

98

6

A special link word feature connects the entries in the dictionary. These are words that, when you look them up in the dictionary, extend the meaning of the original word. The use of link words helps to encourage an understanding that many mathematical ideas are connected. At end of the book there are useful lists giving apparatus, months of the year, days of the week, everyday instruction words, position and direction words, chance and money words, and mathematical symbols, tables, and formulae. There is an alphabetical index to make finding words easy.

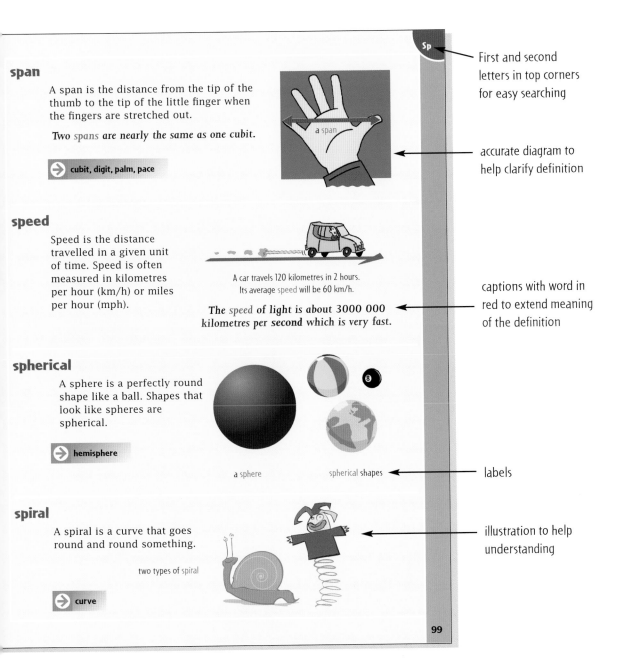

Sp

First and second letters in top corners for easy searching

span

A span is the distance from the tip of the thumb to the tip of the little finger when the fingers are stretched out.

Two *spans* are nearly the same as one cubit.

→ cubit, digit, palm, pace

a span

accurate diagram to help clarify definition

speed

Speed is the distance travelled in a given unit of time. Speed is often measured in kilometres per hour (km/h) or miles per hour (mph).

A car travels 120 kilometres in 2 hours. Its average speed will be 60 km/h.

The *speed* of light is about 3000 000 kilometres per second which is very fast.

captions with word in red to extend meaning of the definition

spherical

A sphere is a perfectly round shape like a ball. Shapes that look like spheres are spherical.

→ hemisphere

a sphere   spherical shapes

labels

spiral

A spiral is a curve that goes round and round something.

two types of spiral

→ curve

illustration to help understanding

accurate

accuracy

1. When you are accurate you are exactly right without any mistakes or errors.

2. When you use measuring instruments you measure to a certain accuracy. For example, to the nearest millimetre, gram, or millilitre.

2 cm long

This measurement is accurate to the nearest cm.

acute angle

An acute angle measures between 0° and 90°.

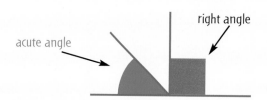

acute angle

right angle

angle, degree,
obtuse angle,
right angle

Acute angles are less than a right angle.

acute-angled triangle

An acute-angled triangle has all three angles less than a right angle.

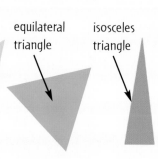

equilateral
triangle

isosceles
triangle

scalene
triangle

obtuse-angled triangle,
right-angled triangle

Acute-angled triangles can be equilateral, isosceles, or scalene.

AD

The letters AD mean *Anno Domini*. AD is used in dates to show the number of years after the birth of Christ.

In the year 1088AD the first mechanical clock was built in China.

 BC

addition +

add, added to, adding

Addition is combining two or more numbers together to make a new number called the sum.

The sign for addition is +. This is called the plus sign.

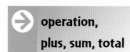 operation, plus, sum, total

$$4 + 7 = 11$$

The *sum* of 4 and 7 is 11.
Four *plus* seven equals eleven.
Four *add* seven equals eleven.
7 *added* to 4 makes 11.
The *total* of 4 and 7 is 11.
Adding 7 to 4 totals 11.

These are all the same addition.

adjacent

Adjacent means lying next to, or side by side.

These two angles are adjacent to each other.

 parallel

afternoon

The time between noon and evening is called the afternoon.

 evening, morning, p.m.

3:00 p.m.

three o'clock in the afternoon

algorithm

An algorithm is the method you use to work out the answer to a calculation.

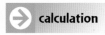 calculation

$$53 \times 5$$

multiply the tens first:
$$50 \times 5 = 250$$

then multiply the units:
$$3 \times 5 = 15$$

then total the two parts:
$$250 + 15 = 265$$

a.m.

The letters a.m. stand for *ante meridiem*, which is Latin for 'before noon'. The letters are used to show times after 12 midnight but before 12 noon.

3:00 a.m.

three o'clock in the morning

 morning, night, p.m.

analogue

Analogue clocks and watches have hands that tell the time.

 digital

Analogue watches have hands.

Digital watches only have numbers.

angle

An angle is an amount of turn. Angles can be measured in degrees.

These angles have been measured in degrees:

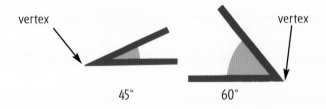

vertex

vertex

45°   60°

acute angle, degree, obtuse angle, right angle, vertex

anticlockwise

Anticlockwise is turning the opposite way to the hands of a clock.

clockwise, rotate

apex

plural *apexes*

The apex of a shape is the point that is furthest away from the base.

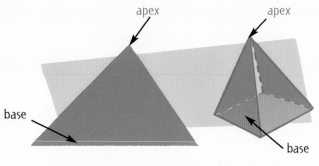

apex

apex

base

base

2D and 3D shapes have apexes.

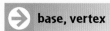 base, vertex

approximate ≈

approximation, approximating, approximately

An approximate number or measurement is near enough the exact answer. Similar words to approximate are nearly, round about, and near enough. The sign for an approximation is ≈.

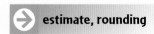 estimate, rounding

3.99 metres is approximately 4 metres

$$3.99 \text{ m} \approx 4.00 \text{ m}$$

£200.01 is approximately £200

$$£200{\cdot}01 \approx £200$$

arc

An arc is part of the circumference of a circle or any curve. You can draw arcs with compasses.

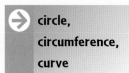 circle, circumference, curve

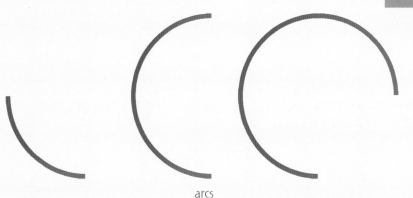

arcs

area

The area of a shape is how much surface it has. Area is measured in square units such as square centimetres (cm^2), square metres (m^2), and square kilometres (km^2).

Both shapes have an area of 2 cm².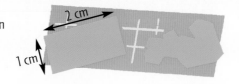

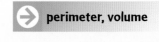 perimeter, volume

arithmetic

Arithmetic is working with numbers. It includes adding, subtracting, multiplying, and dividing with whole numbers, fractions, and decimals.

 calculation, operation

If you are good at arithmetic you will be able to work out the answers to these calculations in your head.

34 + 67   24 × 5

72 - 39   120 ÷ 4

ascending

Ascending means going up or increasing in size.

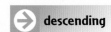 descending

2   6   16   29   45

These numbers are in ascending order.

attribute

An attribute is a property such as colour, shape, size, number of sides, type of angle.

 property

The attributes these shapes have in common include: colour, right-angled, straight-sided.

The attributes they do not have in common include: number of sides, area, symmetry.

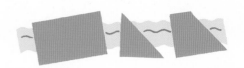

average

In a range of numbers the average is the typical or middle value. There are different types of average called mean, median, and mode.

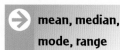

→ **mean, median, mode, range**

Here are five numbers ranging from 3 to 9:

3 3 4 6 9

The mean is 5 because $\frac{3+3+4+6+9}{5}$ equals 5.

The median is 4 because it is the middle value.

The mode is 3 because it occurs most often.

axis

plural *axes*

1. Many graphs have two axes: a horizontal axis and a vertical axis.
2. An axis is a straight line through the middle of a 3D shape.

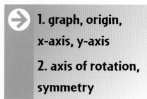

→ **1. graph, origin, x-axis, y-axis**

2. axis of rotation, symmetry

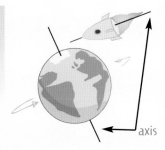

axis

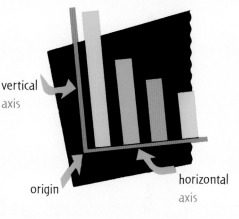

vertical axis

origin

horizontal axis

axis of rotation

An axis of rotation is a straight line through the middle of a 3D shape around which the shape turns. The Earth turns on its axis.

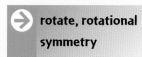

→ **rotate, rotational symmetry**

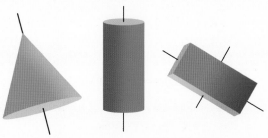

Some axes of rotation on 3D shapes.

Bb

balance

1. A balance is an instrument for weighing or comparing masses or weights.
2. A balance is the amount of money that is still owing or how much remains.
3. An equation balances when one side equals the other.

a balance

If you have £100 in the bank and withdraw £20 the balance is £80.

$3 + b = 12$
For this equation to balance, b must equal 9.

→ 1. scale
2. interest
3. equation

bar chart

A bar chart is a graph that uses bars to show information. The bars are all the same thickness and can be horizontal or vertical.

→ **axis, bar-line graph, block graph, graph**

This bar chart has vertical bars.

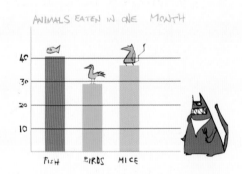

ANIMALS EATEN IN ONE MONTH

FISH   BIRDS   MICE

bar-line graph

A bar-line graph is a graph that has lines instead of bars to show information. The lines can be horizontal or vertical.

→ **bar chart, graph**

This bar-line graph has horizontal line bars.

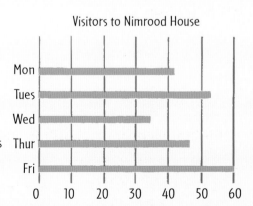

Visitors to Nimrood House

Mon
Tues
Wed
Thur
Fri

0   10   20   30   40   50   60

base

1. The base of a shape is the part on which it stands. It is usually the horizontal part but not always.

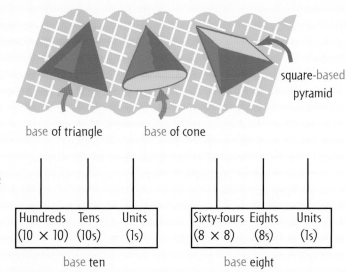

square-based pyramid

base of triangle   base of cone

2. Our number system is called base 10 because we use 10 digits to record all our numbers. Base 2 numbers would only use the digits 0 and 1.

Hundreds (10 × 10)	Tens (10s)	Units (1s)

base ten

Sixty-fours (8 × 8)	Eights (8s)	Units (1s)

base eight

 1. pyramid   2. place value

BC

The letters BC mean 'before Christ'. BC is used in dates to show the number of years before the birth of Christ.

 AD

The ancient Egyptians used a very accurate calendar in 3000 BC.

bearing

A bearing is an amount of turn measured from North in a clockwise direction. Bearings are used with maps to work out travelling directions.

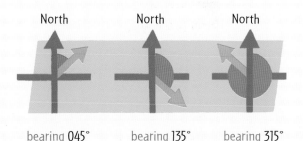

North   North   North

bearing 045°   bearing 135°   bearing 315°

 compass points

billion

A billion used to be a million million but now is more often used to mean a thousand million.

million

1 000 000 000 000   *a million million*
1 000 000 000   *a thousand million*

bisect

When you bisect something, you cut it in half.

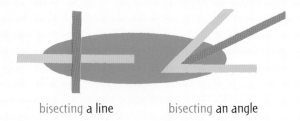

bisecting a line   bisecting an angle

block graph

A block graph is made up of blocks. The blocks are usually square.

 bar chart, graph

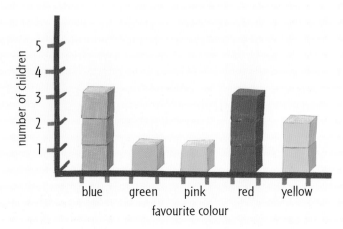

The blocks can be horizontal or vertical.

brackets ( )

Brackets tell you which part of a calculation to work out first.

$$12 - (7 - 3)$$

$$12 - \quad 4 \quad = 8$$

$$(2 \times 3) + 4$$

$$6 \quad + 4 = 10$$

 calculation, operation

breadth

The breadth is the distance from one side to the other. It is sometimes called the width. When measuring length and breadth, the breadth is usually the shorter length.

length, width

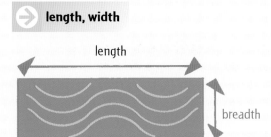

length

breadth

C

The Romans used the letter C to stand for the number 100.

I V X L C D M
Roman numerals

$C = 100$
$CI = 101$
$CV = 105$
$CC = 200$

 Roman numerals

calculation

calculate, calculating
A calculation is when you have to work out the answer to a number problem.

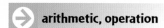 **arithmetic, operation**

Calculate the answer to: $\frac{3}{4}$ of 160.

Answer: 120

calculator

A calculator is a machine that works out calculations very rapidly and accurately.

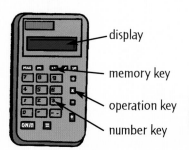
display
memory key
operation key
number key

 operation

calendar

A calendar shows time divided into years, months, weeks, and days.

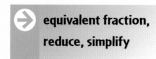 **leap year, month, year**

cancel

cancelling
To cancel a fraction you divide the numerator and denominator by the same number. Cancelling will make smaller numbers to work with.

$\frac{10}{15}\,{}^{2}_{3} = \frac{2}{3}$

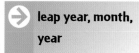 **equivalent fraction, reduce, simplify**

Both numerator and denominator have been divided by 5.

$\frac{10}{15}$ **has been** cancelled **to $\frac{2}{3}$.**

capacity

Capacity is how much something holds. It is usually measured in litres and millilitres.

 litre, millilitre, volume

The capacity of the carton is 1 litre.

Carroll diagram

A Carroll diagram is used for sorting.
One part of the diagram is the opposite of the other.

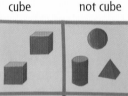

cube   not cube

red

not red

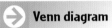 **Venn diagram**

Carroll diagrams are named after the author, Lewis Carroll.

centilitre cl

A centilitre is one hundredth of a litre. There are 10 millilitres in 1 centilitre. *Centi* at the start of a word usually means 'one hundredth'.

$$100 \text{ centilitres} = 1 \text{ litre}$$

$$100 \text{ cl} = 1 \text{ litre}$$

$$1 \text{ cl} = 10 \text{ ml}$$

$$1 \text{ centilitre} = \tfrac{1}{100} \text{ litre}$$

 decilitre, litre, millilitre

centimetre cm

A centimetre is one hundredth of a metre. There are 10 millimetres in 1 centimetre. *Centi* at the start of a word usually means 'one hundredth'.

$$100 \text{ centimetres} = 1 \text{ metre}$$

$$100 \text{ cm} = 1 \text{ m}$$

$$1 \text{ cm} = 10 \text{ mm}$$

$$1 \text{ centimetre} = \tfrac{1}{100} \text{ metre}$$

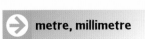 **metre, millimetre**

centre

The centre of a shape is exactly in the middle.

 circle

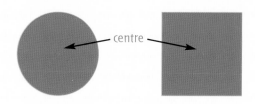
centre

centre of rotation

Shapes can be rotated clockwise or anticlockwise about a point. The point can be inside the shape or outside the shape. This point is called the centre of rotation.

 rotational symmetry

X is the centre of rotation of the rocket.

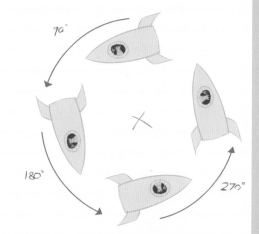

century

A century is a set of one hundred. A century is 100 years.

 Roman numeral , millennium

Roman soldiers were organized into hundreds, they were called centurions.

chart

A chart shows information. Maps are an example of one type of chart.

 tally

This is a tally chart.

How the boys in class 4 come to school

chord

A chord is a straight line that joins two points on the circumference of a circle.

 circumference, diameter, radius

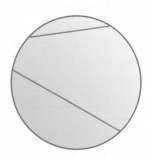

Both lines are chords.

circle

circular

A circle is a 2D shape that is completely round. Something that looks like a circle is circular.

 centre, circumference, diameter, quadrant, radius, semi circle

A circle has different parts.

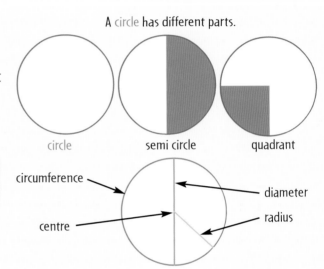

circle   semi circle   quadrant

circumference

diameter

centre

radius

circumference

Circumference is the distance all the way round a circle. It is the perimeter of a circle.

 circle, perimeter

circumference

class interval

A class interval is a range of numbers or values. You sometimes use class intervals when you are collecting information.

 frequency

Children's pocket money in Tiptree School

class interval	frequency
£0.00 to £0.99	7
£1.00 to £1.99	7
£2.00 to £2.99	9
£3.00 to £3.99	18
£4.00 to £4.99	14
£5.00 or more	4

Somebody who had £4.50 pocket money would be in the class interval £4 to £4.99.

clockwise

Clockwise is turning the same way as the hands of a clock.

clockwise   anticlockwise

 anticlockwise, rotation

coin

A coin is money made from metal. Money is also made from paper and called notes. Coins are usually worth less than notes.

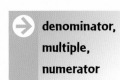

column

A column of numbers is written vertically.

1	2	3	4
5	6	7	8
9	10	11	12
13	14	15	16

a column

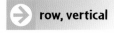 row, vertical

common denominator

A common denominator is a multiple of the denominators of two or more fractions.
Changing fractions to a common denominator allows you to compare, add, and subtract the fractions.

 denominator, multiple, numerator

12 is the common denominator of thirds and quarters. Both $\frac{2}{3}$ and $\frac{3}{4}$ can be changed to twelfths.

compare

comparison, comparing

1. Numbers can be compared in different ways. For example, finding out how much more one number is than another.

2. Comparison is important in measurement. You may need to compare two items to find the heaviest or longest and by how much.

Compare 20 and 2000.
How many times greater is one than the other?

Compare these two lengths:

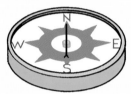

A

B

How many mm longer is one than the other?

Answers: 100 times greater
19 mm longer

compass

A compass is an instrument used to find direction. The needle on a compass always points to the north.

→ **compass points**

compass points

There are four main compass points called NORTH, SOUTH, EAST, and WEST. These are called the cardinal points of a compass.

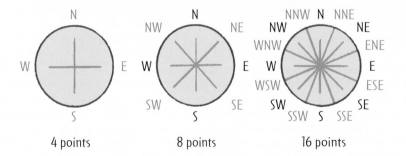

4 points   8 points   16 points

→ **bearing**

There are compass points between N, S, E, and W such as NE, SW, NNE, WSW.

compasses

Compasses are an instrument used to draw circles or arcs.

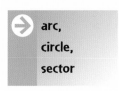
→ arc, circle, sector

complement

A complement is what is needed to make something complete.

30 and 70 are complements of 100.

20° and 70° are complements of a right angle.

$\frac{1}{4}$ and $\frac{3}{4}$ are complements of 1.

concave

Concave means curved inwards like a cave.

→ convex

concentric

Shapes that are concentric have a centre that is in common. A bullseye target is made up of concentric circles.

→ centre

concentric circles   concentric squares

cone

conical

A cone has a flat base that is a circle. The top comes to a point and its sides are curved. Conical shapes look like cones.

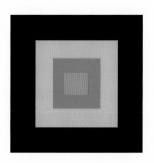

→ apex, base

cone   conical shapes

consecutive

Consecutive means one after the other in a regular order.

14, 15, 16, 17 are consecutive **whole numbers.**

7, 9, 11, 13 are consecutive **odd numbers.**

1, 4, 9, 16 are consecutive **square numbers.**

construct

When you construct a shape you draw it very accurately using instruments such as ruler, compasses, protractor, set square.

You should use a sharp pencil when constructing.

convert

conversion, converting
When you convert something you change it from one thing into another. You can use conversion graphs and tables when converting between units.

120 cm converts **into 1.2 metres.**

5°C converts **into 41°F.**

convex

Convex means curved outwards. Convex is the opposite of concave.

 concave

coordinates

Coordinates are two numbers or letters that describe a position on maps, graphs, and charts. The horizontal coordinate is always written first and the vertical coordinate second.

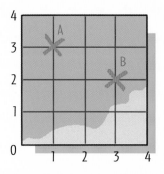

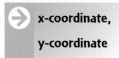 **x-coordinate,**

y-coordinate

The coordinates of A are (1,3).

The coordinates of B are (3,2).

correct

correction

1. When something is correct it is accurate, proper, or right. Correct is the opposite of incorrect.

2. If you correct something you make it right by removing the error. A correction is what you do to make a mistake right.

$3 \times 4 = ?$

The correct answer is 12.

error $\quad 3 \times 4 = 14$ ✗

correction $\quad 3 \times 4 = 12$ ✓

cost price

Cost price is what a person pays to buy something. A manufacturer's cost price is a shopkeeper's buying price. The shopkeeper adds on a profit and sells it to a customer.

 loss, profit

A shopkeeper buys an item for £75 (cost price).

The shopkeeper sells the item for £100 (selling price).

The shopkeeper's profit is £25.

The shopkeeper's selling price is the customer's cost price.

cross-section

A cross-section is a cut straight across a 3D shape. It is a slice of an object.

prism

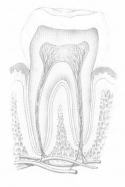

A cross-section of a tooth.

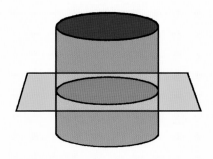

The cross-section of a cylinder is a circle.

cube

cubed

1. A cube is a 3D shape shaped like a box, with six square faces. A cube has 6 faces, 8 vertices, and 12 edges.
2. The cube of a number is the number multiplied by itself three times. The cube of four is 4 × 4 × 4.

All these are cubes.

→ 1. cuboid, face

2. cube root, square number

Seven cubed is 7 × 7 × 7 which is written as 7^3.

cube root $\sqrt[3]{}$

The cube root of a number is that number which, multiplied by itself three times, gives the number to be cube rooted.

The cube root of 27 is 3 because 3 × 3 × 3 = 27.

The cube root of 27 is written as $\sqrt[3]{27}$.

The cube root of 125 is 5 because 5 × 5 × 5 = 125.

The cube root of 125 is written as $\sqrt[3]{125}$.

→ cube, square root

cubic centimetre cm^3

A cubic centimetre is used to find the volume of containers or objects. A cubic centimetre is the space taken up by a 1 cm cube. The short way of writing cubic centimetre is cm^3.

Volume = 8 cubic centimetres or 8 cm^3.

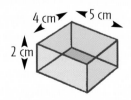

4 cm   5 cm

2 cm

→ cubic metre, volume

Volume = 5 × 4 × 2 cubic centimetres or 40 cm^3.

cubic metre m³

A cubic metre is used to find the volume of quite large containers or objects. A cubic metre is the space taken up by a 1 metre cube. The short way of writing cubic metre is m³.

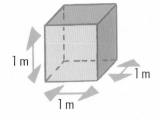

Volume = 1 cubic metre or 1 m³.

 cubic centimetre, volume

cubit

A cubit is the distance from the tip of the middle finger to the elbow. The Ancient Egyptian Royal Cubit was made from granite and divided into 7 palms and 28 digits. It was one of the very first standard units of measurement.

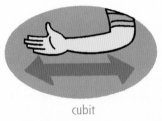

cubit

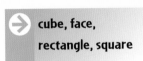 **digit, palm, standard unit**

cuboid

A cuboid is a 3D shape shaped like a box, with six rectangular faces. A cuboid has 6 faces, 8 vertices, and 12 edges.

 cube, face, rectangle, square

All these are cuboids.

Some cuboids have one pair of square faces.

curve

A curve is a bend. Curves can be lines or surfaces.

 arc, edge, line, surface

a curved line   A cone has a curved surface.

cylinder

cylindrical

A cylinder is a 3D shape shaped like a roller. It has two flat faces and one curved surface. Cross-sections of a cylinder are all identically sized circles.

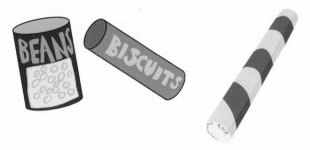

Cylindrical shapes are shaped like cylinders.

 cross-section, face

Dd

D

The Romans used the letter D to stand for the number 500.

I V X L C D M

Roman numerals

D = 500
DL = 550
DC = 600

 Roman numerals

data

Data is information or facts you find out or are given. Data can be words, numbers, or a mixture of both.

A telephone directory is full of data about names, addresses, and telephone numbers.

 database

database

A database is a large amount of information often stored in a computer. You can use the database to sort the information in different ways.

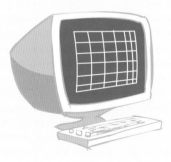

Bookshops use a database to store information such as author, publisher, publication date, price, reference number.

 data

date

Dates can be used to tell you when something happened or will happen. Usually a date tells you the day, month, and year. History dates often only use the year.

 calendar

25th May 1943
This date shows day, month, and year.

16.04.2004
This date is the 16th of April in the year 2004.

William Shakespeare 1564–1616
This date shows the years Shakespeare was born and died.

decagon

A decagon is any 2D shape that has 10 straight sides. If all the sides and angles are the same size it is a regular decagon.

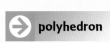 polygon

a regular decagon

decahedron

plural *decahedra*
A decahedron is any 3D shape that has 10 flat faces. *Dec* at the start of a word often means 'ten'.

 polyhedron

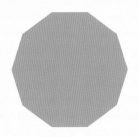

An octagonal prism is an example of decahedron.

decilitre dl

A decilitre is one tenth of a litre. There are 100 millilitres in 1 decilitre. *Deci* at the start of a word usually means 'one tenth'.

$$1 \text{ dl} = \tfrac{1}{10} \text{ litre} \qquad 1 \text{ litre} = 10 \text{ decilitres}$$

$$10 \text{ dl} = 1 \text{ litre} \qquad 1 \text{ litre} = 100 \text{ centilitres}$$

$$1 \text{ dl} = 10 \text{ cl} \qquad 1 \text{ litre} = 1000 \text{ millilitres}$$

$$1 \text{ dl} = 100 \text{ ml}$$

 centilitre, litre, millilitre

29

decimal fraction

A decimal fraction is a sort of fraction that uses tenths, hundredths, thousandths, and so on. Decimal fractions have digits to the right of the decimal point.

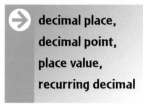

decimal place,
decimal point,
place value,
recurring decimal

$$0.5 = \tfrac{5}{10} = \tfrac{1}{2} \qquad 0.25 = \tfrac{25}{100} = \tfrac{1}{4} \qquad 0.125 = \tfrac{125}{1000} = \tfrac{1}{8}$$

Decimal fractions **use the decimal point.**

decimal number

You use decimal numbers when you use hundreds, tens, and units. Decimals are based on ten, multiples of ten, and tenths. A decimal point separates whole numbers from decimal fractions.

124.75
This decimal number **is made up of:**

1 hundred
2 tens
4 units or ones
7 tenths
5 hundredths

decimal fraction,
decimal place,
decimal point, digit,
place value

decimal place

Decimal place is the number of digits after the decimal point. You sometimes have to write numbers to a certain number of decimal places.

12.56 has 2 decimal places.

0.228 has 3 decimal places.

0.00675 has 5 decimal places.

3.234677 written to 2 decimal places is 3.23

decimal point,
digit,
rounding

decimal point

A decimal point is used to separate the whole numbers from the fractions in a decimal number. It comes between the units digit and the tenths digit.

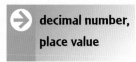
decimal number, place value

This number says forty-two point six.

42.6
↑
decimal point

6.45 m
Measurements also use the decimal point.

decimetre dm

A decimetre is one tenth of a metre. There are 10 centimetres in one decimetre. *Deci* at the start of a word usually means 'one tenth'.

$10 \text{ dm} = 1 \text{ metre}$

$10 \text{ cm} = 1 \text{ dm}$

$1 \text{ decimetre} = \frac{1}{10} \text{ metre}$

centimetre

a decimetre

decrease

When you decrease something you make it less or smaller.

Decrease **65** *by* **15.**
The answer is 50.

subtraction

deep

Deep is how far down or back something goes. You can have deep water or a deep cave.

breadth, depth, shallow

DEEP

degree

1. Degree is a unit used to measure the size of angles. A complete turn measures 360º.
2. Degree is a unit used to measure temperature. There are different types of degrees. The most common are degrees Celcius ºC and degrees Fahrenheit ºF.

This angle measures 45 degrees.

We write this as 45˚.

Using Celcius degrees:
water boils at 100˚C and freezes at 0˚C.

Using Fahrenheit degrees:
water boils at 212˚F and freezes at 32˚F.

➜ **angle, bearing**

denominator

The bottom number of a fraction is called the denominator.
The denominator tells you how many equal parts the quantity or shape has been separated into.

numerator

$$\frac{2}{3}$$

denominator

➜ **common denominator, fraction, numerator**

depth

Depth is a measure of deepness. It is the distance down or back.

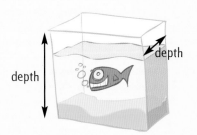

depth

The depth of the tank is from front to back.

The depth of the water is from the surface to the bottom.

➜ **breadth, deep**

descending

Descending means going down or reducing in size.

74 66 42 30 23
These numbers are in descending order.

➜ **ascending**

diagonal

A diagonal is a straight line that joins any two corners of a shape. Diagonals do not always cut a shape in half or go through the middle.

 diameter

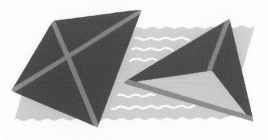

A diagonal can be outside the shape.

diagram

A diagram is a drawing or picture used to make something clear or simple.

This diagram shows two types of cylinder.

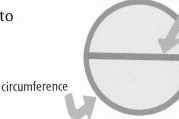 **Carroll diagram, plan, Venn diagram**

diameter

Any straight line from one side of a circle to the other is called a diameter. It must go through the centre.

 centre, circle, circumference, radius

diameter

circumference

diamond

A diamond is another name for a rhombus. It is a four-sided shape without right angles. All four sides are the same length.

 polygon, quadrilateral, rhombus

diary

A diary is a book in which you keep daily records of what has happened.

 **calendar**

difference

The difference is the amount one quantity is greater or less than another. You find the difference by subtracting the smaller number from the larger number.

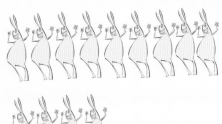

The difference is 5.

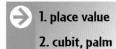
→ subtraction

digit

1. There are ten digits. They are 0, 1, 2, 3, 4, 5, 6, 7, 8, and 9. These digits are used to build up other numbers.
2. A digit is a measurement that is the same as the width of your forefinger.

27 is a 2-digit number.

235 is a 3-digit number.

1067 is a 4-digit number.

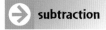
→ 1. place value
2. cubit, palm

digital

A digital clock or watch has only numbers on it instead of a dial and hands.

→ analogue

Analogue watches have hands.

Digital watches only have numbers.

dimension

Dimensions are measurements of size such as length, width, height, and radius.

 measure, size

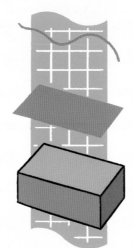

A line has one dimension, length.

A plane shape has two dimensions, length and breadth.

A solid shape has three dimensions, length, breadth, and height.

discount

A discount is a reduction in the cost of something. You often get a discount for paying early or buying in large quantities.

FULL PRICE ₹200
DISCOUNT PRICE ₹175.
YOU SAVE ₹25.

 decrease, percent, reduction

distance

Distance tells you how far apart two things are. The shortest distance between two places is a straight line. Distances are measured in units such as centimetres, metres, and kilometres.

The distance between the towns by road is greater than the distance in a straight line.

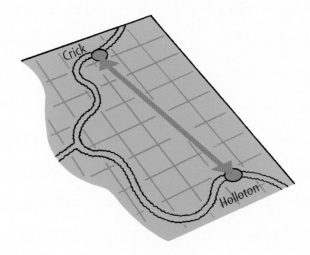

Crick

Holloton

divide

dividing, divided by
When you divide you share things equally.

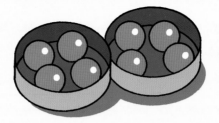

→ division, remainder, share

8 divided by two equals 4. $8 \div 2 = 4$

dividend

1. Dividend is the quantity that has to be divided.
2. Dividend is what you receive as interest on money you have invested.

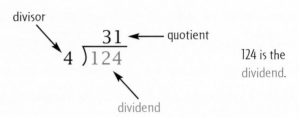

divisor

31 ← quotient

4)124

dividend

124 is the dividend.

Invest £100.

Receive a dividend 5p for each £1.

Total £105.

→ 1. divisor, quotient
2. interest

divisibility rules

Divisibility rules are quick checks to see whether one number will divide exactly into another.

Some divisibility rules:

- All even numbers are divisible by 2.
- All numbers that end in 5 or 0 are divisible by 5.

→ dividend, divisor, quotient

divisible

One number is divisible by another number if the remainder is zero.

→ dividend, divisor, quotient, remainder

$$45 \div 9 = 5$$

45 is divisible by 9 because there is no remainder.

$$48 \div 9 = 5 \ r3$$

48 is not divisible by 9 because there is a remainder.

division ÷

1. Division is sharing things equally.
2. Division is grouping into sets of the same size.

> dividend, divisor, quotient, remainder, share

The sign for division is ÷.

1. **Division by sharing things equally:**
   What is 8 divided by 2?
   $$8 \div 2 = 4$$

2. **Division by grouping into sets of the same size:**
   How many twos are in 8?
   $$8 \div 2 = 4$$

divisor

A divisor is a number that is divided into another.

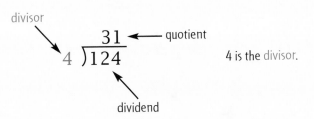

divisor

quotient

4)124

4 is the divisor.

dividend

> dividend, divisor, quotient

dodecahedron

A dodecahedron is a 3D shape that has 12 flat faces. A regular dodecahedron has 12 pentagon faces.

a regular dodecahedron

> regular polyhedron, pentagon

double

Double is twice as many.

Double **15** is **30**.

> treble, triple

37

edge

The edge of a shape is where two faces meet. An edge can be straight or curved.

 face, vertex

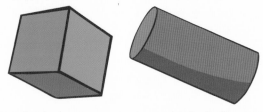

A cube has 12 straight edges.

A cylinder has 2 curved edges.

ellipse

An ellipse is like a flattened circle. It has two lines of symmetry.

 oval

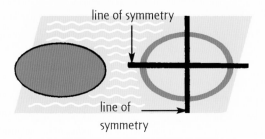

line of symmetry

line of symmetry

enlarge

If you enlarge something you make it bigger. The opposite of enlarge is reduce.

 reduce, scale

The small picture has been enlarged.

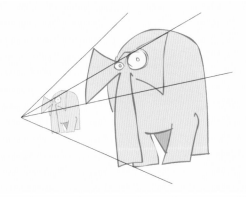

equal

1. Two things are equal if they are the same in some way.
2. Numbers or calculations are equal when they are worth the same.

A

B

The rods are equal in length but have different thickness and colour.

3 + 4 and 10 − 3 are equal because both have an answer of 7.

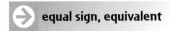 **equal sign, equivalent**

equal sign =

The equal sign is used to show equal quantities or numbers. It was first used by Robert Recorde in 1557.

 equation

$$3 \times 4 = 12$$

$$100 \text{ cm} = 1 \text{ metre}$$

$$3 + y = 10$$

equation

An equation has two parts separated by an equal sign. The left part of an equation is always worth the same as the right part.

 equal sign

Here are some equations:

$$5 + [\ ] = 9$$

$$12 - y = 3$$

$$2b + 4 = b + 7$$

equilateral triangle

An equilateral triangle has all its sides the same length. Each of its three angles is also the same.

 angle, triangle

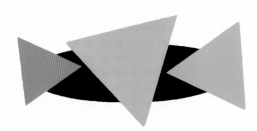

Each angle in an equilateral triangle is 60°.

equivalent

Equivalent means worth the same. Equivalent things may look different but they always have the same value.

 equal, equivalent fraction

is equivalent to

is equivalent to

$$3 \times 8 \longrightarrow 4 \times 6$$

equivalent fraction

Equivalent fractions are worth the same. When you cancel a fraction the new fraction is equivalent to the original fraction.

$$\frac{4}{6} = \frac{2}{3}$$

$$\frac{3}{4} = \frac{75}{100}$$

equivalent fractions

 cancel, fraction

$$\frac{\cancel{10}^{\,2}}{\cancel{15}_{\,3}} = \frac{2}{3}$$

Cancelling makes an equivalent fraction.

Eratosthenes sieve

Eratosthenes was a Greek mathematician who lived between 275 and 195 BC. He found a way of finding prime numbers using the Sieve of Eratosthenes.

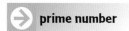 prime number

To find prime numbers up to 100 using the Sieve of Eratosthenes:

- Cross out 1.
- Cross out multiples of 2 but not 2.
- Cross out multiples of 3 but not 3.
- Cross out multiples of 5 but not 5.
- Cross out multiples of 7 but not 7.

The numbers not crossed out are prime numbers.

estimate

estimation

When you make an estimate you judge the amount without measuring or calculation. A guess is different to an estimate. When you guess you do not have any idea of the answer.

 guess

Answer: between 10 cm and 14 cm is a good estimate.

What is your estimation of the length of this line in cm?

even

An even number is any whole number that can be divided by 2 exactly.

$2, 18, 56, 176, 3086$

All these are even numbers.

divisible, odd, prime number

evening

Evening comes after the afternoon. It is the end of the daytime. We often talk about early evening and late evening.

9:00 p.m.

nine o'clock in the evening

 afternoon, morning

exact

When something is exact it is neither more nor less. When you measure exactly you measure very accurately.

The rods are exactly the same length.

 accurate

exchange

When you exchange something you change it for something else. Usually the things you exchange are worth the same.

The money can be exchanged for the stamp.

 Ff

face

A face is the side of a solid shape. It usually means flat faces. The base of a shape is also a face.

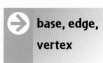 base, edge, vertex

This pyramid has 5 faces.

factor

A factor is a whole number that will divide exactly into another number.

 divisor, multiple

3 is a factor of 21.

7 is a factor of 63.

2 and 7 are both factors of 14.

fathom

A fathom is the distance between fingertip and fingertip of outstretched arms. A fathom is a standard unit of six feet (1.83 m). It was used to measure the depths of oceans.

 cubit

Sailors used a weighted rope marked with fathoms.

figure

A figure is a number used to write an integer.

The number twenty-six in figures is 26.

 digit, number, numeral

flat

Flat means smooth and level.

 curved line   flat line

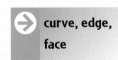 curve, edge, face

flat angle

A flat angle is two right angles together. It is an angle of 180°.

 angle, right angle

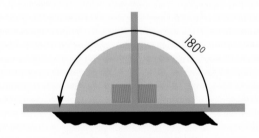

A flat angle measures 180°.

flat shape

A flat shape is very thin. 2D shapes are sometimes called flat shapes.

 two-dimensional

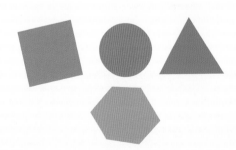

flip

When you flip something you turn it over to its other side.

→ reflect, rotate

foot

plural *feet*

A foot is an imperial unit used to measure length. A foot is divided into 12 parts called inches. A foot measures about 30 cm.

$1 \text{ foot} = 12 \text{ inches}$

$3 \text{ feet} = 1 \text{ yard}$

$1 \text{ foot} = 30.48 \text{ cm}$

→ metric units

formula

plural *formulae*

A formula is a shorthand way of writing a rule.

Formula for finding area of a rectangle:
$A = L \times B$

Formula for finding circumference of a circle:
$C = \pi \times D$

→ equation

fraction

Fractions are usually parts of something. The bottom part of a fraction is called the denominator. It tells you the number of equal parts. The top part is the numerator. It tells you the number of those parts you are dealing with.

→ denominator, numerator

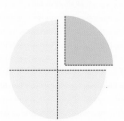

The circle has been divided into four equal parts.

Three parts are light blue and one part dark blue.

$\frac{3}{4}$ is light blue and $\frac{1}{4}$ is dark blue.

fraction as a quotient

A quotient is the result of dividing two numbers. When a larger number is divided into a smaller number the quotient is a fraction.
When one number is not exactly divisible by another the quotient can be written as a mixed number.

$$3 \div 4 = \tfrac{3}{4}$$

When you divide 3 by 4 the quotient is the fraction $\tfrac{3}{4}$.

$$15 \div 4 = 3$$

When you divide 15 by 4 the quotient is $3\tfrac{3}{4}$.

 improper fraction, mixed number, quotient

fraction as a ratio

A fraction can be a ratio between two numbers.

Two out of three apples were bad.

The fraction of bad apples was $\tfrac{2}{3}$.

 proportion, ratio

fraction of a quantity

When you find the fraction of a quantity you divide by the denominator and multiply by the numerator.

$\tfrac{1}{5}$ of $20 = 4$ $\tfrac{1}{4}$ of $12 = 3$

$\tfrac{4}{5}$ of $20 = 16$ $\tfrac{3}{4}$ of $12 = 9$

 division

frequency

Frequency is how often something happens. Tally marks are often used to show the frequency in a frequency chart or diagram.

MARKS	FREQUENCY	
21-25	III	3
16-20	⊦⊦⊦ II	7
11-15	⊦⊦⊦ ⊦⊦⊦	10
6-10	IIII	4
1-5	⊦⊦⊦	5

The frequency diagram shows marks scored in a test.

→ **tally**

gallon

A gallon is an imperial unit used to measure capacity. A gallon is divided into 8 parts called pints. A gallon measures about $4\frac{1}{2}$ litres.

$$1 \ gallon = 8 \ \text{pints}$$

$$1 \ gallon = 4 \ \text{quarts}$$

$$1 \ gallon = 4.55 \ \text{litres}$$

➔ **capacity, imperial units, metric units**

gram g

Grams are metric units of mass used to weigh things. There are 1000 grams in a kilogram. One gram is very light.

$$1000 \ grams = 1 \ \text{kilogram}$$

$$1000 \ g = 1 \ \text{kg}$$

➔ **mass, metric units, weight**

graph

A graph is a picture, chart, or diagram showing information about things.

This graph shows how fast a sunflower grows.

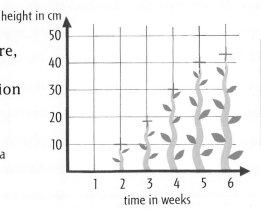

height in cm

time in weeks

➔ **block graph, data, line graph, pictogram, pie chart**

greater than ➤

more than, larger than
You use the words 'greater than' when comparing two unequal numbers. You can also use 'more than' or 'larger than'.

$$12 > 7$$

12 is greater than 7.

➔ **equal, less than, symbol**

grid

A grid is usually two or more sets of parallel lines crossing each other. Most grids are squares but they can be rectangles or triangles.

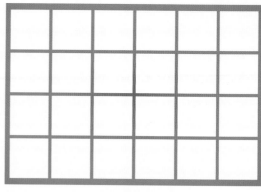

a square grid

grouped data

Sometimes data is grouped together in blocks like these times:

2:30 to 2:59;

3:00 to 3:29;

3:30 to 3:59.

The times between 2:30 and 4:00 are grouped together in half hour blocks.

The class interval of the grouped data is half an hour.

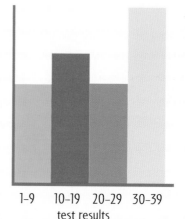

1–9   10–19   20–29   30–39
test results

The test marks have been grouped into tens.

The test marks are grouped data.

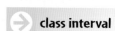 class interval

guess

A guess is when you try to state a number, quantity, or measurement without having any information to help you. When you estimate you have information to help in the estimation.

 estimate

Guess what I had for my birthday.

There is no information available to help the guessing.

Hh

half

plural *halves*
A half is one of two equal parts. You can find half of a shape, quantity, or number.

Half of 25 is 12½.

Half of the shape is coloured.

Half of the 16 squares is coloured.

 fraction, halve, quarter

halve

halving
If you halve something you divide it into two equal pieces. Halving a number is the same as dividing it by two.

halving an orange

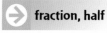 **fraction, half**

height

1. Height is how tall something is.
2. Height is the vertical distance from the ground.

height of the boy   height of the kite

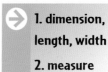 **1. dimension, length, width 2. measure**

hemisphere

A hemisphere is half a sphere. It has one flat face which is a circle.

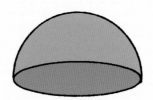

hemisphere

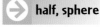 **half, sphere**

heptagon

heptagonal

A heptagon is any polygon that has 7 straight sides. A regular heptagon has all its sides and angles equal. Heptagonal shapes have 7 sides.

regular heptagon   irregular heptagon

 polygon, regular polygon, two-dimensional

hexagon

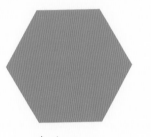

hexagonal

A hexagon is any polygon that has 6 straight sides. A regular hexagon has all its sides and angles equal. Hexagonal shapes have 6 sides.

regular hexagon   irregular hexagon

 polygon, regular polygon, two-dimensional

hexagonal prism

A prism that has hexagon ends is called a hexagonal prism.

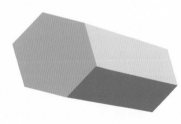

 polyhedron, prism

hexagonal prism

hexahedron

plural *hexahedra*

A hexahedron is any solid shape that has 6 flat faces.

 polyhedron, three-dimensional

Both cubes and cuboids are hexahedra.

hexomino

plural hexominoes
A shape made from arranging six identical squares together is called a hexomino. The squares are joined at their sides.

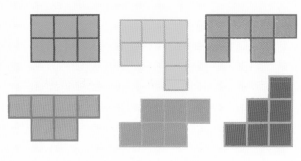

some hexominoes

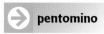 **pentomino**

highest common factor HCF

The highest common factor is the largest number that divides into a set of numbers without leaving a remainder. The initials HCF mean highest common factor.

 factor, lowest common multiple

8, 12, 20

Four is the largest number that will divide exactly into all these numbers.

The highest common factor of 8, 12, and 20 is 4.

The HCF of 8, 12, and 20 is 4.

hollow shape

A shape that has nothing inside is hollow.

 solid

a hollow pentagonal prism

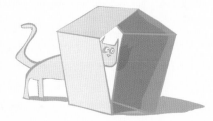

horizontal

A horizontal line is parallel to the horizon or ground. A table has a horizontal top.

 vertical

horizontal line

vertical line

hour

An hour is a measurement of time. There are 24 hours in one day. An hour is divided up into minutes and seconds.

1 hour has passed.

$$1 \text{ hour} = 60 \text{ minutes}$$

$$1 \text{ hour} = 3600 \text{ seconds}$$

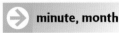 **minute, month**

Ii

I

The Romans used the letter I to stand for the number 1.

I V X L C D M
Roman numerals

$$I = 1$$
$$II = 2$$
$$III = 3$$
$$IIII = 4$$

 Roman numerals

IV

Sometimes the Roman numeral 4 is written as IV instead of IIII. When I is placed before another letter you subtract one from the value of the letter.

$IV = 4$ (1 before 5)

$XIV = 14$ (10 and 1 before 5)

$LIV = 54$ (50 and 1 before 5)

$CIV = 104$ (100 and 1 before 5)

 Roman numerals

IX

Sometimes the Roman numeral 9 is written as IX instead of VIIII. When I is placed before another letter you subtract one from the value of the letter.

$IX = 9$ (1 before 10)

$XIX = 19$ (10 and 1 before 10)

$LIX = 59$ (50 and 1 before 10)

$CIX = 109$ (100 and 1 before 10)

 Roman numerals

icosahedron

plural *icosahedra*
An icosahedron is a 3D shape that has 20 flat faces. A regular icosahedron has 20 faces that are identical equilateral triangles.

 equilateral triangle,
polyhedron,

a regular icosahedron

identical

When two or more shapes are identical they have the same shape, size, and colour.

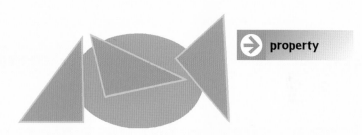 property

Identical shapes can be in different positions.

imperial units

Imperial units are measurements such as feet and inches, pints and gallons, pounds and ounces. They have been largely replaced by metric units.

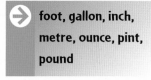 foot, gallon, inch,
metre, ounce, pint,
pound

Length

12 inches = 1 foot

3 feet = 1 yard

1760 yards = 1 mile

Mass

16 ounces = 1 pound

14 pounds = 1 stone

112 pounds = 1 hundredweight

20 hundredweight = 1 ton

Capacity

8 pints = 1 gallon

improper fraction

An improper fraction has a numerator larger than its denominator. It is a fraction that is worth more than one.

$$\frac{7}{3}$$

This is an *improper fraction*.

→ denominator, mixed number, numerator, vulgar fraction

inch

An inch is an imperial unit used to measure length. Twelve inches measure the same as one foot. An inch measures about $2\frac{1}{2}$ cm.

12 inches $= 1$ foot

1 inch $= 2.54$ cm

→ foot, metre

increase

When you increase something you make it more or larger.

Increase **65** by **15**.

→ add

Answer: 80

inequality < > ≠

An inequality is when two numbers are not worth the same. The symbols used to show inequality are < > and ≠.

$12 > 9$

12 is greater than 9

$56 < 62$

56 is less than 62

$4 + 6 \neq 9$

4 + 6 does not equal 9

All these are *inequalities*.

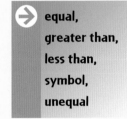

→ equal, greater than, less than, symbol, unequal

infinity ∞

Infinity means going on forever. The counting numbers go on forever, they never stop. Counting goes on to infinity. The symbol for infinity is ∞.

0, 1, 2, ...345, ...12 780, ...53 667 867, ...∞

Counting numbers go on forever to *infinity*.

integer

An integer is any whole number. An integer can be a positive or a negative number. Zero is also an integer.

negative integers   positive integers

0 is also an integer.

interest

interest rate

Interest is payment for using money. If you borrow money you pay interest. If you lend money you receive interest. Interest is usually written as a percentage called the interest rate.

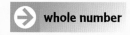 **percent**

Borrow £100.

5% interest rate.

Repay £105,
the interest paid is £5.

Lend £100.

12% interest rate.

Receive £112,
the interest received is £12.

intersect

intersection, intersecting

Lines intersect when they cross each other. Where they cross is called the intersection. Intersecting lines can be straight or curved.

Intersection of two lines.

These arcs are intersecting in two places.

interval

An interval is the amount of time or space between two things.

6, 9, 12, 15

The interval between these numbers is 3.

inverse

1. If you turn something upside down you have its inverse.
2. Inverse means to reverse something. Addition and subtraction are inverse operations. Multiplication and division are also inverse operations. The inverse undoes the previous calculation.

The inverse of $\frac{3}{4}$ is $\frac{4}{3}$.

The inverse of $+ 7$ is $- 7$.

$$17 + 7 - 7 = 17$$

The inverse of $\times 4$ is $\div 4$.

$$17 \times 4 \div 4 = 17$$

irregular polygon

An irregular polygon does not have all its sides the same length. Some might be the same but not all of them.

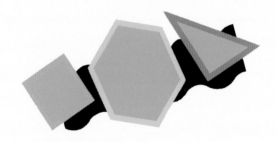

irregular polygons

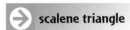
regular polygon

isosceles triangle

An isosceles triangle has two sides that are the same length. Two angles are also equal.

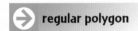
scalene triangle

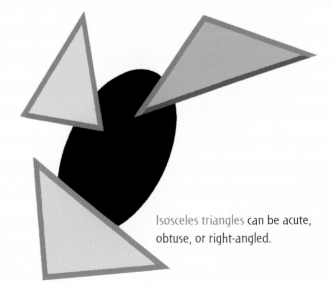

Isosceles triangles can be acute, obtuse, or right-angled.

Jj

join

When you join two points you draw a straight line between them.

A and B have been joined.

junction

A junction is where two or more lines meet.

→ **intersect, vertex**

A is the junction of the two lines.

Kk

kilogram kg

A kilogram is a metric unit of mass used for weighing. There are 1000 grams in 1 kilogram. *Kilo* at the start of a word often means '1000'.

1 kg weighs about the same as 10 large eating apples.

→ **gram, metric units, tonne**

kilometre km

A kilometre is a metric unit of length used to measure long distances. There are 1000 m in 1 km.

It takes about 10 minutes to walk 1 km.

→ **metre, metric units, speed**

kite

A kite is a 4-sided polygon. It has two pairs of adjacent sides that are the same length. One pair of angles is the same size.

kites

→ **adjacent, polygon, quadrilateral, two-dimensional**

L

The Romans used the letter L to stand for the number 50.

I V X L C D M

Roman numerals

L = 50
LII = 52
LV = 55

 Roman numerals

label

When you label something you give it a name. A label tells you what something is. A title is a sort of label.

 axis, graph

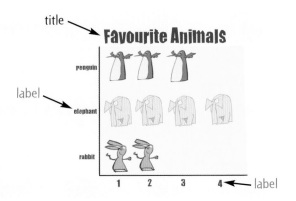

title → **Favourite Animals**

penguin

label → elephant

rabbit

1   2   3   4 ← label

leap year

A leap year has 29 days in February. This happens every fourth year. There are 366 days in a leap year. Leap years happen because it takes approximately $365\frac{1}{4}$ days for the earth to orbit the Sun, not 365 days.

1972, 2000, 2004, 2116
These dates are leap years.

Usually if you can divide the year exactly by 4 it is a leap year.

 calendar, date, month, year

length

1. Length is the measurement along a line or curve. When you measure the length and width of something the length is usually the longer distance.

2. You can measure the length of time in seconds, minutes, hours, days, weeks, months, and years.

The length of each line is 5 cm.

5 seconds is a short length of time.
150 years is a long length of time.

 1. breadth, dimension, height, width

2. time

less than ‹

Less than means 'not so many as' or 'fewer than'. It also means 'smaller than'. The symbol for less than is <. The smaller number always comes before the symbol.

$$15 < 20$$
Fifteen is *less than* twenty.

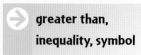

greater than, inequality, symbol

line

Usually a line is used to mean a straight line. However a line can also be curved. If you are asked to draw a line between two points always draw a straight line.

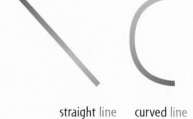

straight line   curved line

curve, intersect, parallel

line of symmetry

A line of symmetry divides a shape in half. One half is the reflection of the other half. The line of symmetry is the same as a mirror line. Some shapes have no lines of symmetry, others have one or more.

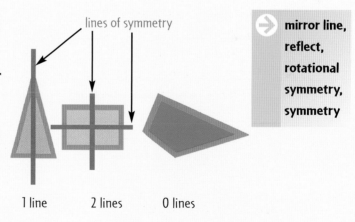

lines of symmetry

1 line   2 lines   0 lines

mirror line, reflect, rotational symmetry, symmetry

list

When you make a list you write things underneath each other. Sometimes you put a list in an order.

a shopping list

litre l

A litre is a metric unit used to measure capacity or volume. It is usually used for measuring liquids.

$1 \ litre = 1000 \ millilitres$

$1 \ litre = 100 \ centilitres$

$1 \ litre = 10 \ decilitres$

 centilitre, decilitre, metric units, millilitre

loop

A loop is something that bends round. A loop often returns to its starting point.

a loop   loops making a pattern

loss

A shopkeeper makes a loss when the selling price is less than the buying price.

Price paid to buy an item £10.

Price received selling the item £8.

Loss £2.

lowest common multiple LCM

The lowest common multiple of two numbers is the smallest number that is a multiple of both numbers. The initials LCM mean lowest common multiple.

 highest common factor, multiple

Multiples of 6 are
6, 12, 18, 24, 30, ...

Multiples of 8 are
8, 16, 24, 32, 40, ...

Common multiples of 6 and 8 are
24, 48, 72, ...

The lowest common multiple is 24.

Mm

M

The Romans used the letter M to stand for the number 1000.

I V X L C D M
Roman numerals

M = 1000
MD = 1500
MCCXV = 1215
MM = 2000

 Roman numerals

magic square

In a magic square all the numbers in each row, column, and diagonal have the same total.

4	3	8
9	5	1
2	7	6

→ **column, diagonal, row**

In this magic square each row, column, and diagonal totals 15.

mapping

map

A mapping is when you join two sets. You map each member of one set to a member of the second set using a rule.

→ **rule**

These are mappings:

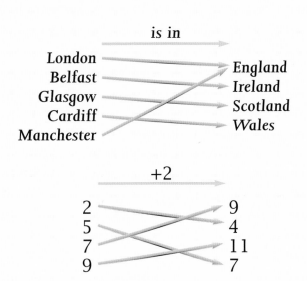

mass

Mass is the amount of matter or material in an object. An elephant has more mass than a cat. Mass and weight are closely linked but are not quite the same. Weight is the measurement of the force of gravity on an object. Many books use the word 'weight' to mean the same as 'mass'. Metric units of mass are grams, kilograms, and tonnes.

An astronaut's mass is the same on Earth as on the Moon.

An astronaut will weigh less on the Moon than on Earth.

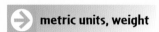 metric units, weight

maximum

The maximum is the largest number in a set. Maximum is the largest possible size, amount, or value.

19°C 23°C 21°C 18°C

The **maximum** temperature was 23°C.
This was the highest temperature that was recorded.

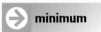 minimum

mean

Mean is a kind of average. There are different types of average called mean, median, and mode. To find the mean, total the quantities then divide by the number of quantities.

Here are five numbers ranging from 3 to 9:

3 3 4 6 9

The total is $3 + 3 + 4 + 6 + 9$.

The mean is $\frac{3+3+4+6+9}{5}$.

The mean average is 5.

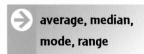 average, median, mode, range

measure

measurement

A measure is the size of something using a measuring unit. The measuring units are usually metric or imperial. When you have measured something you record the measurement. Measurements include grams, metres, seconds, and degrees.

James measured Lisa's height.

The measurement was 97 cm.

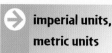
imperial units, metric units

median

1. Median is a kind of average. There are different types of average called mean, median, and mode. To find the median, write out the quantities in order. The median is the quantity that has the middle value.
2. Median is the special name given to a line drawn from a corner of a triangle to the middle of the opposite side.

Here are five numbers ranging from 3 to 9:

3 3 4 6 9

The median is 4 because it is the middle value.

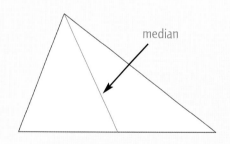
median

1. average, mean, mode, range
2. equilateral, isosceles, scalene, triangle

metre m

A metre is a metric unit used to measure length or distance.

$$1 \text{ metre} = 1000 \text{ millimetres}$$
$$1 \text{ metre} = 100 \text{ centimetres}$$
$$1 \text{ metre} = 10 \text{ decimetres}$$
$$1000 \text{ metres} = 1 \text{ kilometre}$$

centimetre, decimetre, kilometre, metric units, millimetre

metric ton

A metric ton is 1000 kilograms. A metric ton is often called a tonne.

$$1000 \text{ kilograms} = 1 \text{ tonne}$$

A tonne is the same as a metric ton.

 kilogram, metric units, tonne

metric units

Metric units are part of the metric system of measurement. The units are based on tens, hundreds, and thousands. Metric units started to be used at the time of the French Revolution.

→ centimetre, gram, kilogram, kilometre, litre, metre, millilitre, millimetre

Length	Mass	Capacity
millimetre	gram	millilitre
centimetre	kilogram	centilitre
decimetre	tonne	decilitre
metre		litre
kilometre		

mid

Mid is short for middle. Words such as midday, midsummer, and midpoint all have something to do with middle.

 midday, midnight

C is the midpoint between A and B.

Midday is 12:00 or noon.

Midsummer day is June 24th.

midday

Midday is the middle of the day. It is another name for noon. Midday happens 12 hours after midnight. Midday is the time when a.m. times become p.m. times.

 a.m., midnight, p.m.

midnight

Midnight is the middle of the night. Midnight happens 12 hours after midday. Midnight is the time when p.m. times become a.m. times. Using a 24 hour clock midnight is 24:00 or 00:00; both these are correct.

 a.m., midnight, p.m.

mile

Mile is an imperial unit used to measure long distances. The distance got its name from the Latin *mille passus* which meant a thousand paces. It takes about 15 minutes to walk 1 mile. 1 mile is approximately 1500 m.

$$1 \text{ mile} = 1760 \text{ yards}$$

$$1 \text{ mile} = 1479.5 \text{ metres}$$

$$5 \text{ miles} \approx 8 \text{ kilometres}$$

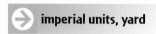 **imperial units, yard**

millennium

A millennium is one thousand years.

The year 2000 was the second millennium AD.

The year 3000 will be the third millennium AD.

 AD, BC, century

millilitre ml

A millilitre is a metric unit used to measure a small capacity or volume. There are 1000 millilitres in 1 litre. A teaspoon holds about 5 ml.

$$1000 \text{ millilitres} = 1 \text{ litre}$$

$$100 \text{ millilitres} = 1 \text{ decilitre}$$

$$10 \text{ millilitres} = 1 \text{ centilitre}$$

 centilitre, decilitre, litre, metric units

millimetre mm

A millimetre is a metric unit used to measure a small length or distance. There are 1000 mm in 1 m.

1000 millimetres = 1 metre

100 millimetres = 1 decimetre

10 millimetres = 1 centimetre

 centimetre, metre, metric units

million

A million is a large number. It is one thousand thousands. You write it as one followed by six zeros. A million is a seven digit number.

1 million = 1 000 000

 billion, digit, place value

minimum

The minimum is the smallest number in a set. Minimum is the smallest possible size, amount, or value.

-1°C   -3°C   0°C   -2°C

The minimum temperature was -3°C.

This was the lowest temperature that was recorded.

 maximum

minus −

Minus is the name for the subtraction symbol −.

8 − 5 = 3

Eight minus five equals three.

 plus, symbol

minute

minute hand

A minute is a measurement of time. There are 60 minutes in 1 hour. A minute can be divided up into 60 seconds. A clock has a minute hand and an hour hand.

60 minutes = 1 hour

60 seconds = 1 minute

10 minutes past 6

analogue, hour

mirror line

A mirror line is a line of symmetry. One half of the mirror line is the reflection of the other half. If you fold along the mirror line one half will fold exactly on top of the other half.

 line of symmetry, reflect, symmetry

1 line of symmetry

2 lines of symmetry

no lines of symmetry

The dotted lines are mirror lines or lines of symmetry.

mixed number

A mixed number is a whole number with a fraction.

$2\frac{1}{2}$ is a mixed number.

 improper fraction, proper fraction, vulgar fraction

mode

Mode is a kind of average. There are different types of average called mean, median, and mode. The mode is the quantity or number that occurs most often.

Here are five numbers ranging from 3 to 9:

3 3 4 6 9

The mode is 3 because it occurs most often in the results.

 average, mean, median, range

month

There are twelve months in one year. A calendar month has 28, 29, 30, or 31 days.

 calendar, year

The 12 months are:

January, February, March, April, May, June, July, August, September, October, November, December.

One month from 25th May is 25th June.

morning

The time between midnight and midday is called the morning. Morning times are a.m. times.

9:00 a.m.

nine o'clock in the morning

 afternoon, a.m., evening

multiple

A multiple is lots of the same number or quantity. Multiples are like multiplication tables. The sixth multiple of 7 is 42.

Multiples of 3 are
3, 6, 9, 12, 15, …

Multiples of 5 are
5, 10, 15, 20, 25, …

multiples of 4

Multiples of 12 are
12, 24, 36, 48, 60, …

 lowest common multiple, multiply

Multiples do not stop at the tenth they go on and on.

multiplication ✗

Multiplication is adding lots of the same number together. The multiplication symbol is ×.

Here are six lots of 5
$5 + 5 + 5 + 5 + 5 + 5 = 30$

This is the multiplication of 5 by 6.
$5 \times 6 = 30$

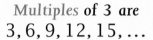 multiple, multiply

multiply ✗

multiplied, multiplying
When you multiply you increase something a number of times. Multiplying is the same as multiplication.

Multiply 4 by 3 means 4 × 3.

$4 \times 3 = 12$

Four multiplied by three equals twelve.

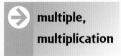 multiple, multiplication

Nn

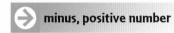

near

nearly

When something is near it is very close to something. Other words that can mean the same as near are close to, nearly touching, next to, almost.

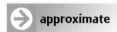
→ **approximate**

The two shapes are near to each other.

48 is near 50.
48 is nearly 50.

negative number

Negative numbers are less than zero. On a number line they are to the left of zero. Negative numbers have the minus sign in front of them.

negative numbers   positive numbers

-4 -3 -2 -1 0 1 2 3 4

You can write negative 2 as -2 or ⁻2.

→ **minus, positive number**

net

A net is a flat shape that you can fold up to make a solid shape. The net shows what a shape looks like once it has been opened out and flattened.

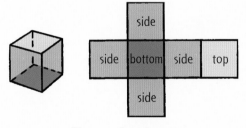

The net of a cube.
A cube has several different nets.

→ **flat shape, solid**

night

Night is the dark part of the day. It is the time between sunset and sunrise.

Midnight is in the middle of the night.

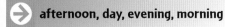
→ **afternoon, day, evening, morning**

nonagon

A nonagon is any 2D shape that has 9 straight sides. A regular nonagon has all its sides and angles the same size.

 irregular polygon, plane shape, polygon

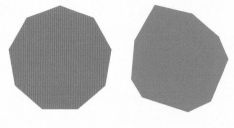

regular nonagon   irregular nonagon

none

None means not one, nothing at all.

 zero

Tom has four oranges but Jo has none.

nought 0

Nought is another word for zero, nothing, or none. The symbol for nought is 0.

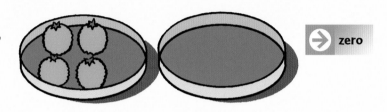

negative numbers   positive numbers

Nought *separates negative and positive numbers.*

3050   0.005

Noughts *are important in place value.*

 place value, zero

number

We use numbers to count quantity or to measure. Numbers have a position on a number line. There are many different kinds of number: whole number, negative number, positive number, integer, decimal number, fractional number, square number, triangle number, prime number.

Counting numbers: 0, 1, 2, 3, 4, 5, 6 ...
Square numbers: 1, 4, 9, 16, 25 ...
Triangle numbers: 1, 3, 6, 10, 15 ...
Prime numbers: 2, 3, 5, 7, 11 ...

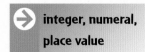 **integer, numeral, place value**

number sentence

A number sentence is a mathematical sentence. It uses numbers, words, and symbols.

 equation

6 subtract 4 leaves 2.

[ ] + 5 = 14

8 > 3

These are all number sentences.

numeral

A numeral is any symbol or word for a number.

 digit, number, Roman numerals

3 three |||

These are all numerals.

numerator

The top number of a fraction is called the numerator. The numerator tells you how many equal parts there are.

numerator

$\dfrac{2}{3}$

denominator

 **denominator, fraction**

There are two thirds.

Oo

oblique

Oblique lines are sloping or slanting. The lines are not horizontal or vertical.

 horizontal, vertical

oblique lines

oblong

An oblong is a shape that is longer than it is wide. Rectangles can be oblongs.

 polygon, quadrilateral, rectangle

an oblong rectangle

an oblong with rounded corners

obtuse angle

An obtuse angle measures between 90° and 180°.

→ acute angle,
angle,
degree,
right angle

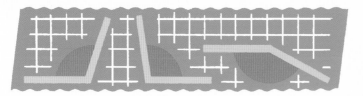

Obtuse angles are between 1 and 2 right angles.

obtuse-angled triangle

An obtuse-angled triangle has one angle greater than a right angle.

→ acute-angled triangle,
right-angled triangle

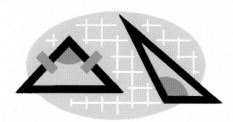

Obtuse-angled triangles can be isosceles or scalene.

octagon

octagonal
An octagon is any polygon that has 8 straight sides. A regular octagon has all its sides and angles equal. Octagonal shapes have 8 sides.

→ irregular polygon, polygon, regular polygon, two-dimensional

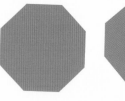 

regular octagon   irregular octagon

octahedron

plural *octahedra*
An octahedron is any solid shape that has 8 flat faces. A regular octahedron has 8 equilateral triangle faces.

→ polyhedron,
regular polyhedron,
solid

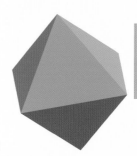

regular octahedron

odd

An odd number is any whole number that cannot be divided by 2 exactly. An odd number is a whole number that is not even.

3, 17, 59, 171, 3089
All these are odd numbers.

 divisible, even, prime numbers

operation + − x ÷

An operation is when you change a number by adding, subtracting, multiplying, or dividing. The operation symbols are + − × and ÷.

$$12 + 5 \qquad 12 \times 4$$

$$12 - 8 \qquad 12 \div 6$$

All these are operations on the number 12.

 add, divide, multiply, subtract

order

You often put things in order of size or quantity. The alphabet is an order for letters.

2, 6, 13, 17, 22
ascending order

 ascending, descending, ordinal

30 cm, 21 cm, 19 cm, 10 cm, 8 cm
descending order

ordered pair

Coordinates are ordered pairs. They are often written in brackets. The order of the two numbers is very important. In an ordered pair (2,3) is different to (3,2).

These ordered pairs are at different positions:

(2,3) *is 2 along and 3 up.*

(3,2) *is 3 along and 2 up.*

order of symmetry

The order of symmetry of a shape is the number of times it will fit into its outline when being rotated.

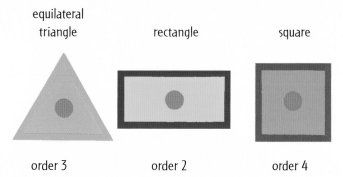

equilateral triangle

rectangle

square

order 3

order 2

order 4

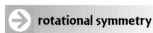 **rotational symmetry**

ordinal

Ordinal numbers are numbers such as first, second, third, fourth. An ordinal number tells you the position of something.

Ordinal **numbers are** **sometimes written like this:**

1st 2nd 3rd 4th 5th.

origin

The origin is where something starts. On a graph the origin is where the two axes cross.

 **coordinates,**
x-axis,
y-axis

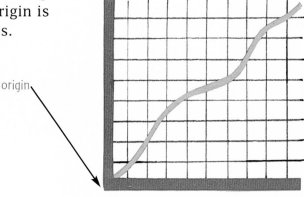

origin

ounce oz

An ounce is an imperial unit of weight or mass. The short way of writing ounce is oz. 1 oz is about 25 gms.

16 *ounces* $= 1$ *pound*

16 *oz* $= 1$ *lb*

1 *ounce* $= 28.3$ *grams*

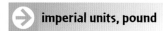 **imperial units, pound**

oval

An oval is a 2D shape like a flattened circle. There are two types of oval. One oval is egg-shaped with one end more pointed than the other. The other oval is called an ellipse.

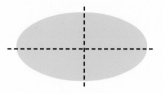

→ **ellipse, symmetry**

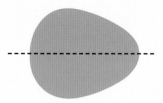

This oval is egg-shaped with 1 line of symmetry.

This oval is an ellipse with 2 lines of symmetry.

ovoid

An ovoid is a 3D shape shaped like an egg. It is like a squashed sphere.

 → **three-dimensional**

an ovoid

Pp

pace

A pace is the distance from heel to toe when walking normally.

a pace

pair

A pair is two of anything.

a pair of shoes

palm

A palm is the width of a hand.
It does not include the thumb.

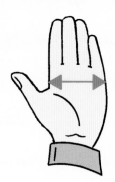

A palm measures
4 finger widths.

parallel

Parallel lines are the same distance apart no matter how long they are. Parallel lines can never cross each other.

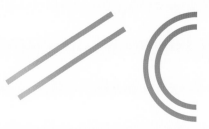

parallelogram

Parallel lines can be straight or curved.

parallelogram

A parallelogram is a 4-sided shape that has its opposite sides parallel to each other.

rectangle,
rhombus

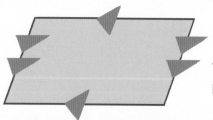

The arrowheads show which sides are parallel to each other.

pattern

A pattern is an arrangement of numbers, lines, or shapes that follows a rule.

square numbers,
tessellate,
triangle numbers

1 **4** 9 16 **25**

pattern of square numbers

tessellating pattern of hexagons

repeating pattern

pentagon

pentagonal

A pentagon is any 2D shape with 5 straight sides. A regular pentagon has all its sides and angles the same. Something that looks like a pentagon is pentagonal.

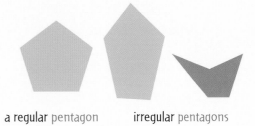

a regular pentagon   irregular pentagons

 polygon, regular polygon, two-dimensional

pentomino

A pentomino is a shape made from arranging 5 identical squares together. The squares are joined at their sides.

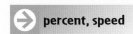 hexomino

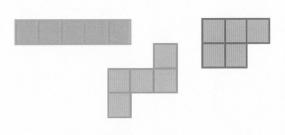

some pentominoes

per

Per means 'for each'. A percentage is a number telling how many are in each hundred.

A speed of 70 kilometres per hour means the vehicle is travelling 70 kilometres in each hour.

£150 per annum = £150 in each year.

£5 per person means each person gets £5.

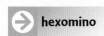 percent, speed

percent %

percentage

Percent means out of a hundred. A percentage is another way of writing a fraction that has a denominator of 100. The symbol for percent is %.

$50\% = \frac{50}{100} = \frac{1}{2}$

$25\% = \frac{25}{100} = \frac{1}{4}$

$10\% = \frac{10}{100} = \frac{1}{10}$

Percentages can be written as fractions.

equivalent fraction, per

perimeter

The perimeter is the distance all the way round a shape.

 circumference

perpendicular

Two things are perpendicular when they meet at right angles.

 horizontal, vertical

Perpendicular lines meet at 90°.

pi π

Pi is just bigger than 3. It is the number you get when you divide the circumference of a circle by its diameter. This always comes to the same number. More accurately pi is 3.142 or $\frac{22}{7}$. The symbol for pi is π.

$$\frac{circumference}{diameter} = \pi$$

$$\frac{circumference}{diameter} = 3.142$$

$$Circumference \ of \ a \ circle = \pi \times D$$

$$Area \ of \ a \ circle = \pi \times r^2$$

 circumference

pictogram

pictograph, picture graph

 block graph

In a pictogram pictures are used to stand for quantities. A picture can stand for one thing or a number of things. Pictograms can be called pictographs or picture graphs.

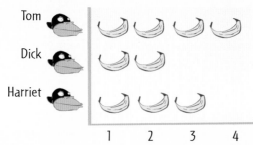

This pictogram shows how many bananas each chimpanzee eats for breakfast. Each picture stands for one banana.

pie chart

In a pie chart information is shown as a circle. The different-sized slices of the pie chart stand for the quantities.

sector

pint

A pint is an imperial unit used to measure capacity. Eight pints make a gallon. A pint is between a half and three quarters of a litre. A litre is about $1\frac{1}{4}$ pints.

$$8 \text{ pints} = 1 \text{ gallon}$$

$$1 \text{ pint} = 0.568 \text{ litres}$$

gallon, imperial units

place value

Place value is the value a digit has because of its position in a number. The same digit can have different values depending on its position in a number.

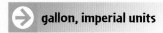
decimal

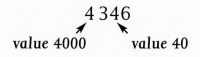

value 4000   value 40

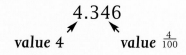

value 4   value $\frac{4}{100}$

plan

A plan is a diagram showing where things are. Often plans have a scale because they cannot be drawn life size.

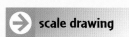
scale drawing

This is a street plan.

plane

A plane is a flat surface. It can be vertical, horizontal, or oblique.

→ plane shape, plane symmetry

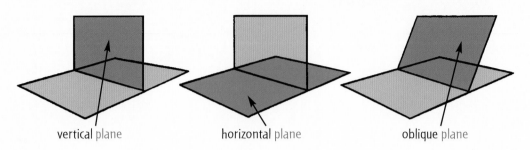

vertical plane   horizontal plane   oblique plane

plane shape

plane figure

Plane shapes are 2D shapes. They have no thickness. Sometimes plane shapes are called plane figures.

Plane shapes can have straight or curved sides.

→ plane, plane symmetry, polygon, two dimensional

plane symmetry

plane of symmetry

Solid shapes can have plane symmetry. Plane symmetry is like mirror symmetry in flat shapes. The shape on one side of the plane must be the reflection of the other side.

→ mirror symmetry, plane, rotational symmetry

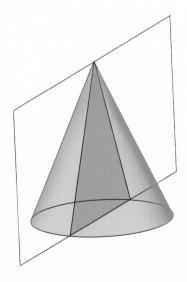

plane of symmetry of a cone

plot

plotting
You plot points on a graph.
When you mark a position
on a graph you are plotting
the coordinates.

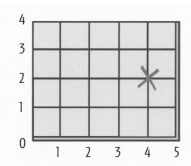

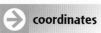
coordinates

The coordinate (4,2)
has been plotted.

plus +

Plus is the name for the
addition symbol +.

$$8 + 5 = 13$$
Eight plus five equals thirteen.

minus,
symbol

p.m.

The letters p.m. stand for *post
meridiem*, which is Latin for 'after
midday'. The letters are used to show
times after 12 noon but before
12 midnight.

9:00 p.m.

nine o'clock in the
evening

afternoon, a.m.

point

1. You plot points on a graph. A point is really
like a very small dot but is often marked with a
small cross. The point is the middle of the cross.
2. A compass has points. The four points of a
compass are N, S, E, and W.

This graph plots the
points (1,3) and (2,2).

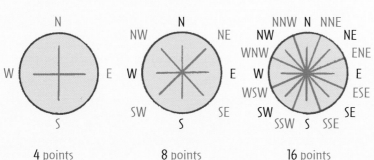

4 points   8 points   16 points

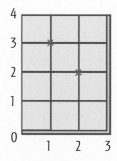
1. coordinate, plot
2. compass points

point symmetry

Point symmetry is when you rotate a shape about a point and it fits into its outline in a different position.

 A

 mirror symmetry, plane symmetry, rotational symmetry

The green triangle will rotate about A to fit exactly onto the yellow triangle.

There is point symmetry about the point A.

polygon

A polygon is any 2D shape with straight sides. Many polygons have special names. For example triangles, squares, and rectangles are types of polygon. Polygons can be regular or irregular.

 concave, convex, plane shape, regular, two-dimensional

polygon sides	special name
3 sides	triangle
4 sides	quadrilateral
5 sides	pentagon
6 sides	hexagon
7 sides	heptagon
8 sides	octagon
9 sides	nonagon
10 sides	decagon

polyhedron

plural *polyhedra*
A polyhedron is any 3D shape made from polygons. Some polyhedra have special names such as cube, pyramid, or tetrahedron. Polyhedra have faces, edges, and vertices.

 edge, face, solid, three-dimensional, vertex

type of face	polyhedron name
4 equilateral triangles	tetrahedron
6 squares	hexahedron or cube
8 equilateral triangles	octahedron
12 pentagons	dodecahedron
20 equilateral triangles	icosahedron

octahedron   dodecahedron   icosahedron

positive number

Positive numbers are more than zero. On a number line they are to the right of zero. Positive numbers have the plus sign in front of them.

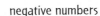 negative numbers   positive numbers

You can write positive 2 as +2 or $^+2$.

 negative number

pound lb £

1. A pound is an imperial unit of weight or mass. The short way of writing pound is lb. A pound is divided into sixteen ounces. A one pound weight is about 450 grams. A kilogram is about $2\frac{1}{4}$ pounds.
2. A pound is an amount of money equal to 100 pennies. The short way of writing a pound is £.

$$1 \text{ } pound = 16 \text{ ounces}$$
$$1 \text{ lb} = 16 \text{ oz}$$

$$1 \text{ lb} = 453.59 \text{ g}$$
$$1 \text{ kg} = 2.204 \text{ lb}$$

$$1 \text{ } pound = 100 \text{ pennies}$$
$$£1 = 100 \text{ p}$$

 1. imperial units, ounce

power

You read 3^4 as three to the power of 4. It means 3x3x3x3. The power shows how many equal numbers have been multiplied together.
A number to the power of 2 is said to be squared. A number to the power of 3 is said to be cubed.

 cube, squared

4^2 is 4 squared or 4 to the power of 2.

4^3 is 4 cubed or 4 to the power of 3.

prime factor

Factors of a number that are also prime numbers are called prime factors.

The factors of 24 are
1, 2, 3, 4, 6, 8, 12, 24.

The prime factors of 24 are 2 and 3.

factor, prime number

prime number

A prime number has only two factors which are 1 and itself. One is not a prime number because it has only one factor not two.

2, 3, 5, 7, 11, 13, 17, 19

These are the prime numbers less than 20.

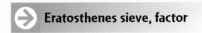 **Eratosthenes sieve, factor**

prism

A prism is a solid shape with matching ends that are polygons. The cross-section of a prism is always the same shape. Cubes and cuboids are special types of prism. A prism is also a polyhedron.

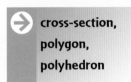 **cross-section, polygon, polyhedron**

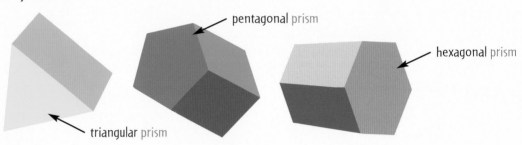

pentagonal prism

hexagonal prism

triangular prism

The shape of the end gives the prism its name.

probability

Probability is the chance of something happening. You often write the probability of something happening as a fraction. Words you might use when talking about probability include: chance, likelihood, odds.

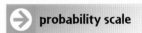 **probability scale**

Toss a coin.

The probability of getting heads is 1 in 2.

The probability is $\frac{1}{2}$.

Roll a dice.

The probability of getting a six is 1 in 6.

The probability is $\frac{1}{6}$.

probability scale

A probability scale is a diagram to show the chance of something happening. If something has no chance of happening, it has a probability of 0. If something is certain, it will have a probability of 1. If something has an even chance, the probability is $\frac{1}{2}$ or 0.5.

A probability scale

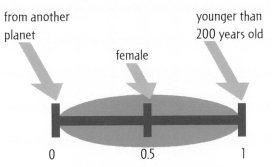

from another planet

female

younger than 200 years old

0   0.5   1

Some information about the first person you might see on the street tomorrow.

 probability

probable

If something is probable it will most likely happen. It might not happen but the chances are that it will.

It is probable *that the next person you meet will be right-handed.*

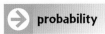 probability

product

The product is the answer you get by multiplying numbers together.

The product **of 3 and 7 is 21 because** $3 \times 7 = 21$**.**

The product **of 2, 4, and 5 is 40 because** $2 \times 4 \times 5 = 40$**.**

 multiply

profit

Profit is what you make when you sell something for more than you paid for it. The profit is the difference between the buying and selling prices.

Buy for £6.

Sell for £10.

Profit is £4.

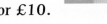 difference

proper fraction

A proper fraction is when the numerator is smaller than the denominator. It is a fraction worth less than 1.

$\frac{7}{8}$ is a proper fraction.

$\frac{4}{3}$ is an improper fraction.

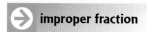 improper fraction

property

properties

You use the property of something when you describe it. Properties are things such as colour, size, number of sides.

 attribute

16

Some properties of this square are: blue, right-angled, equal-sided, four-sided, parallel-sided.

Some properties of this number are: even, square, multiple of 2, factor of 32, less than 20.

proportion

1. A scale model is in proportion to the real thing. With a scale of one fifth everything on the model would be one fifth of the real thing. Maps are in proportion to the real measurements on the ground.
2. Numbers can be in proportion.
2 and 6 are in the same proportion as 5 and 15 because in each pair the first number is a third of the second number.

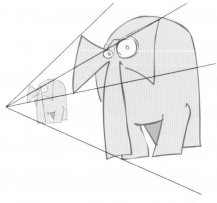

The pictures are in proportion to each other.

1:5 is the same proportion as 2:10 or 3:15.

1. enlargement, reduction, scale

2. equivalent fraction, ratio

pyramid

A pyramid is a solid shape that has a polygon for a base. Each of the sides are triangles meeting at a point. The pyramid with a triangular base is called a tetrahedron.

 polygon, polyhedron, tetrahedron

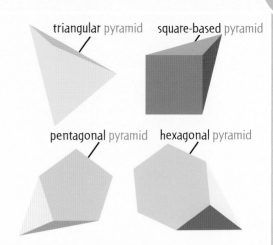

triangular pyramid   square-based pyramid

pentagonal pyramid   hexagonal pyramid

The shape of the base gives the pyramid its name.

Qq

quadrant

1. A quadrant is quarter of a circle. The straight sides are radii of the circle.

2. When you plot coordinates the axes make four quadrants. In the first quadrant both coordinates are positive. In the third quadrant both coordinates are negative.

 1. circle, quarter, radius, semi circle

2. coordinate, negative, positive, x-axis, y-axis

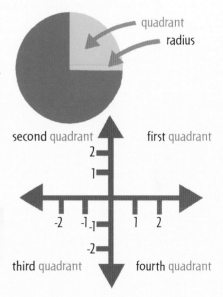

quadrant
radius

second quadrant   first quadrant

third quadrant   fourth quadrant

---

quadrilateral

A quadrilateral is any polygon that has four sides. The four angles of a quadrilateral add up to 360°.

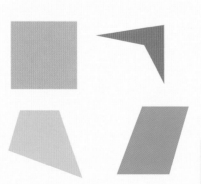

Quadrilaterals have 4 sides and 4 angles.

 polygon, two-dimensional

quart

A quart is an imperial unit used to measure capacity. A quart is a quarter of a gallon. It is the same as two pints.

 gallon, imperial unit, pint

$1 \text{ quart} = 2 \text{ pints}$

$4 \text{ quarts} = 1 \text{ gallon}$

$1 \text{ quart} = 1.14 \text{ litres}$

quarter $\frac{1}{4}$

A quarter is one of four equal parts. You can find a quarter of a shape, quantity, or number. Two quarters is the same as a half.

 equivalent fraction, fraction, half

$\frac{1}{4} \text{ of } 24 = 6$

$\frac{1}{4} \text{ of an hour} = 15 \text{ minutes}$

questionnaire

A questionnaire is a printed set of questions. Questionnaires are used to collect information and data. They often have YES/NO answers, boxes to tick, or scales to show how much you like things.

Questionnaire about reading

Do you read every night? YES/NO

Do you read fiction? YES/NO

Do you read about sport? YES/NO

Do you prefer a paperback to a hardback? YES/NO

quotient

The quotient is the answer to a division. A quotient can be a whole number, fraction, mixed number, or decimal.

 dividend, divisor

$$4\overline{)27}^{\,6\ r3}$$ quotient 6 remainder 3

$$4\overline{)27.00}^{\,6.75}$$ quotient 6.75

$\frac{27}{4} = 6\frac{3}{4}$ quotient $6\frac{3}{4}$

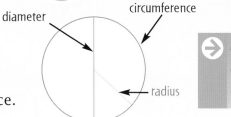

radius

plural *radii*
A radius is any straight
line from the centre of a
circle to the circumference.

diameter

circumference

radius

A radius is half a diameter.

→ **centre, circle, circumference, diameter**

random

randomly
Random means purely by
chance. If you choose a number
at random you pick any number
that you wish. Random
numbers do not have an order.

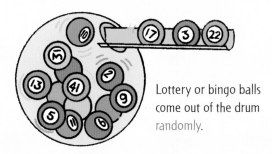

Lottery or bingo balls
come out of the drum
randomly.

range

The range is the difference between
the smallest value and the largest
value. You often need to know the
range when you are finding averages.

Here are five numbers from 3 to 9:

3 3 4 6 9

The smallest number is 3, the largest is 9

The range is from 3 to 9 which equals 6.

→ **average, mean, median, mode**

ratio :

A ratio is when you
compare two numbers
and write one as a
fraction of the other.
We write a ratio of two
to three as 2:3.

James and Tanya share £10 in the ratio 2:3.
This means for each £2 James receives Tanya
will get £3. Altogether James will get £4
and Tanya £6.

A ratio of 2 mm:1 cm can be written differently:
2:10 (both written in mm) or
$\frac{1}{5}$ (as a fraction).

→ **proportion**

rectangle

rectangular

A rectangle is a 2D shape that has 4 straight sides and 4 right angles. The opposite sides of a rectangle are equal. A square is a special type of rectangle. Usually rectangle is used to mean the oblong rectangle.
A rectangular shape is one that looks like a rectangle.

There are two types of rectangle.

square rectangle   oblong rectangle

 oblong, quadrilateral, square

recurring decimal

A recurring decimal is sometimes called a repeating decimal. It is a decimal in which one or more of the digits keeps on repeating itself. Recurring decimals go on and on without end.

 decimal, decimal place

Some recurring decimals:

$\frac{1}{3} = 0.3333333333$ ➡
the digit 3 keeps repeating

$\frac{22}{7} = 3.1428561428561$ ➡
the digits 142856 keep repeating

reduce

When you reduce something you make it smaller. You can reduce quantity and size. The opposite of reduce is enlarge or increase.

If you reduce £7 by £3 the answer is £4.

30 reduced by a half is 15.

£5 reduced by 10% is £4.50.

The picture has been reduced in size.

reduction

Reduction is when you write a fraction in its simplest way. Reduction is the same as simplifying a fraction by cancelling.

 **cancel, equivalent fraction, simplify**

$\frac{8}{12}$ can be reduced to $\frac{2}{3}$

$\frac{6}{15}$ can be simplified to $\frac{2}{5}$

Reduction of fractions is the same as cancelling.

reflect

reflection, reflecting

If you reflect a shape you draw its mirror image. The mirror image is called the reflection. Reflecting a shape swaps left and right over.

 line of symmetry, mirror symmetry , reflective symmetry, symmetry

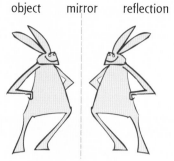

object   mirror   reflection

A reflection is like flipping a shape over.

reflective symmetry

Reflective symmetry is sometimes called mirror symmetry. It is when one half of a shape is the reflection of the other half.

 line of symmetry, mirror symmetry, symmetry

This flower has reflective symmetry. The mirror line is the line of symmetry.

regular polygon

A regular polygon is any polygon that has all its sides and angles the same. A square is a regular quadrilateral.

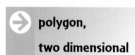 **polygon, two dimensional**

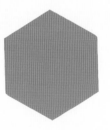

some regular polygons

regular polyhedron

plural *regular polyhedra*

A regular polyhedron is the same as a regular solid. The faces of a regular polyhedron are all identical regular polygons. The faces all meet at the same angle. There are 5 regular polyhedra called tetrahedron, hexahedron, octahedron, dodecahedron, icosahedron.

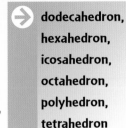
dodecahedron,
hexahedron,
icosahedron,
octahedron,
polyhedron,
tetrahedron

tetrahedron   hexahedron   octahedron   dodecahedron   icosahedron

These are the five regular polyhedra.

remainder r

A remainder is what is left after you share something.

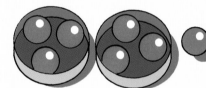

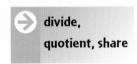
divide,
quotient, share

reverse

Reverse means the opposite way round or in the opposite direction. Addition and subtraction are reverse operations. Multiplication and division are also reverse operations.

inverse, operation

3456

If you reverse the digits you get 6543.

$$12 + 8 - 8 = 12$$

$$12 \times 3 \div 3 = 12$$

If you reverse the operation you undo what you have done.

revolve

revolution

If you revolve something you turn it round. A revolution is a complete turn about a point or axis.

rotate,
turn

The Earth revolves around the Sun.

rhombus

A rhombus has four equal sides. The opposite sides are parallel. It is the correct name for a diamond shape.

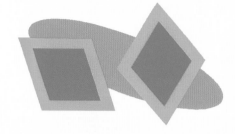

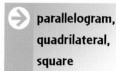
parallelogram, quadrilateral, square

A rhombus looks like a squashed square.

right angle 90°

A right angle is a quarter of a complete turn. It measures 90°.

acute, angle, obtuse

Right angles are often marked with little squares.

right-angled triangle

A right-angled triangle contains one right-angle. Right-angled triangles can be isosceles or scalene.

isosceles, scalene

right-angled triangles

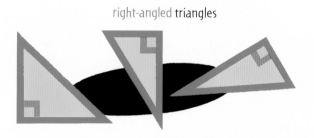

isosceles and right-angled triangle

Roman numerals

The Romans used letters to stand for numbers. They used letters to stand for 1, 5, 10, 50, 100, 500, and 1000.

C, D, I, IV, IX, L, M, V

I	II	III	IV	V	VI	VII	VIII	IX	X
1	2	3	4	5	6	7	8	9	10

XI	XII	XIII	XIV	XV	XVI	XVII	XVIII	XIX	XX
11	12	13	14	15	16	17	18	19	20

XL	L	C	D	M
40	50	100	500	1000

$$MDLXXVI = 1000 + 500 + 50 + 10 + 10 + 5 + 1 = 1576$$

rotate

rotation, rotating

If you rotate something you turn it. A complete rotation is 4 right angles or 360°.

→ **revolve, turn**

The circle is rotating.

rotational symmetry

Rotate a shape in its outline. If it will fit in more than one way it has rotational symmetry. If a shape being rotated looks exactly the same before the turn is complete then it has rotational symmetry.

→ **order of symmetry**

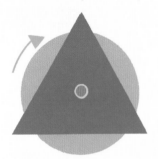

An equilateral triangle fits into its outline 3 times in one rotation.

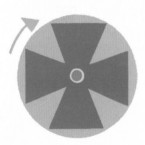

This shape fits into its outline 4 times in one rotation.

This letter fits into its outline twice in one rotation.

round

If something is round it is curved like a circle or sphere.

→ **arc, circle, sphere**

round edges   a perfectly round shape

rounding

round, rounded

Rounding is writing a number as an approximate. Numbers are often rounded to the nearest one, nearest ten, or nearest hundred. Rounding often means round up or round down to the nearest whole unit.

 approximate, decimal places

379 rounded to the nearest hundred is 400.

5.289 rounded to the nearest whole number is 5.

When rounding £136.22 round down to £136.

When rounding 45.8 km round up to 46km.

route

A route is the direction or path taken between two or more places. You can plan a route on a map. You can draw a route on a grid.

The dotted red line shows a route from one island to the other.

row

A row goes horizontally from side to side.

 horizontal

1	2	3	4
5	6	7	8
9	10	11	12

← a row

rule

When you follow a rule you follow the instructions on how to do something. A formula is a shorthand way of writing a rule.

 formula

The rule for finding the area of a rectangle is: multiply the length by the breadth.

ruler

rule

A ruler is a straight edge marked with measurements.
It is used to draw straight lines and to measure lengths.
You rule straight lines with a ruler.

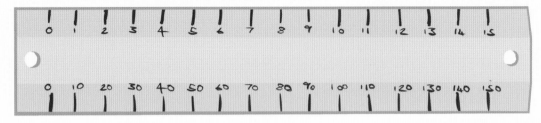

A ruler like this can rule lines in centimetres or millimetres.

Ss

scale

A scale is a set of points on a line used for measuring. You can see a scale on maps, thermometers, measuring jugs, or rulers.

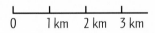

0   1 km   2 km   3 km

scale: 1 cm represents 1 km

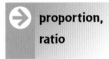
proportion, ratio

scale drawing

A scale drawing is smaller, larger, or the same size as the real thing. Everything on the scale drawing is in proportion to the real thing.

Scale 1:200

enlarge, proportion, reduce

Scale drawing of a small bungalow.
1 cm represents 2 m.

scalene triangle

A scalene triangle has no sides the same length. All its angles are a different size.

→ equilateral, isosceles, triangle

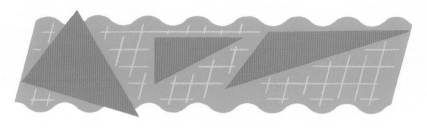

A scalene triangle can be acute, obtuse, or right-angled.

sector

A sector is a slice taken out of a circle. The two straight edges are the radii of the circle and the curved side is an arc. Quadrants and semi circles are types of sector.

→ arc, quadrant, radius, semi circle

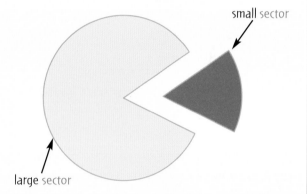

small sector

large sector

segment

A segment is part of a line or a circle. A chord cuts a circle into two segments.

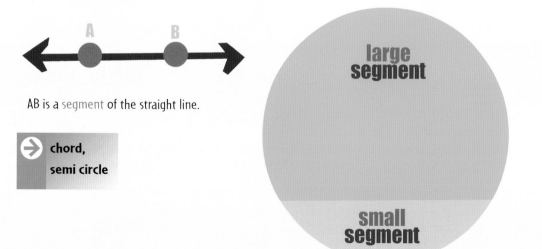

A B

AB is a segment of the straight line.

→ chord, semi circle

large segment

small segment

semi circle

A semi circle is half of a circle. The straight side is a diameter of the circle.

 circle, diameter, half, quadrant

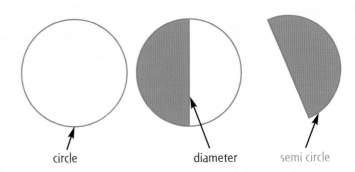

circle   diameter   semi circle

sequence

A sequence is a set of numbers usually written in a line.

 multiple, prime number, square number, triangle number

$3, 6, 9, 12, 15, \ldots$

$1, 4, 9, 16, 25, \ldots$

$2, 6, 18, 54, 162, \ldots$

These are different sorts of sequences.

set

A set is a collection of numbers, shapes, or objects that have something in common.

 attribute, property, subset

a set of triangles

shallow

If something is shallow it does not go down or back a long way.

 deep

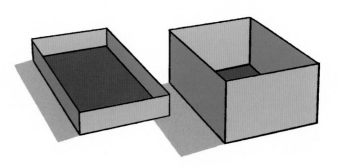

a shallow box   a deep box

share ÷

sharing, shared by

When you share you divide things equally. Sharing is the same as dividing. The symbol for sharing is ÷.

 divide, remainder

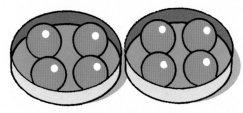

8 shared between two equals 4.

$$8 \div 2 = 4$$

side

1. Some 2D shapes have sides. The sides can be straight or curved.

2. The sides of a shape are not the top, bottom, front, or back. Sides can be left or right.

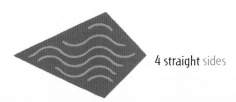

4 straight sides

left side   top   right side

bottom

sign

A sign is a short way of saying something. A sign usually tells you what to do.

 minus, plus, symbols

addition sign +

subtraction sign −

multiplication sign ×

division sign ÷

square root sign √

simplify

simplest

To simplify you write something in a more simple way. Fractions are written in the simplest way when both numerator and denominator are as small as possible.

If you cancel you can simplify $\frac{8}{12}$ to $\frac{2}{3}$:

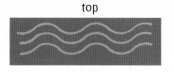

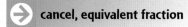 cancel, equivalent fraction

size

Size is the dimensions of an object. Size can be the amount of something. Size can be the weight, volume, or capacity of things.

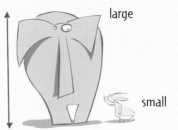

large

small

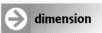

→ dimension

slide

When you slide a shape you move it without turning it or flipping it over. You can slide horizontally, vertically, diagonally, or obliquely.

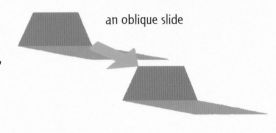

an oblique slide

→ translate

solid

A solid is any shape that has a length, width, and height. A solid has three dimensions. Not all solids have flat faces.

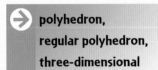

→ polyhedron,
regular polyhedron,
three-dimensional

some solid shapes

solution

solve

A solution is an answer to a problem. When you solve something you find the solution. Sometimes there are several solutions to a problem.

The solution to $(3 \times 4) - 2$ is 10.

If you solve the equation $y + 7 = 10$

the solution is $y = 3$.

span

A span is the distance from the tip of the thumb to the tip of the little finger when the fingers are stretched out.

Two spans are nearly the same as one cubit.

 cubit, digit, palm, pace

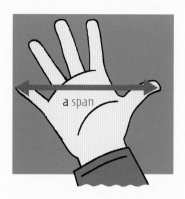

a span

speed

Speed is the distance travelled in a given unit of time. Speed is often measured in kilometres per hour (km/h) or miles per hour (mph).

A car travels 120 kilometres in 2 hours.
Its average speed will be 60 km/h.

The speed of light is about 3 000 000 kilometres per second which is very fast.

sphere

A sphere is a perfectly round shape like a ball. Shapes that look like spheres are spherical.

hemisphere

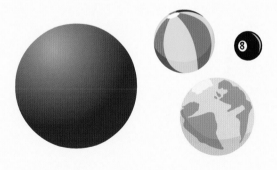

a sphere   spherical shapes

spiral

A spiral is a curve that goes round and round something.

two types of spiral

 curve

square

1. A square is a four-sided shape with all its sides and angles the same size.
2. The square of a number is when you multiply the number by itself.

Squares can be filled in or just be an outline.

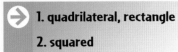

1. quadrilateral, rectangle

2. squared

Square 3 *and the answer is* 9.

square-based pyramid

A square-based pyramid has a face that is square. The other four sides are triangles that meet at a point.

The base of a shape can be turned to the top.

base, polyhedron, pyramid

square centimetre cm^2

A square centimetre is a unit used to measure area. It is an area that is the same as that of a 1 cm square. A square centimetre can be written as cm^2.

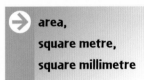

area, square metre, square millimetre

A 1 cm square has an area of 1 cm^2.

This shape also has an area of 1 square centimetre.

squared

When a number is squared, it is multiplied by itself. Whole numbers, fractions, and decimals can be squared.

square, square number

6 *squared is* $6 \times 6 = 36$

$$6^2 = 36$$

2.5 *squared is* $2.5 \times 2.5 = 6.25$

$$2.5^2 = 6.25$$

square metre m²

A square metre is a unit used to measure large areas. It is an area that is the same as that of a 1 m square. A square metre can be written as m².

1 *square metre* = 10,000 *square centimetres*

$$1 \text{ m}^2 = 10{,}000 \text{ cm}^2$$

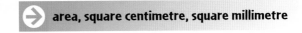 **area, square centimetre, square millimetre**

square millimetre mm²

A square millimetre is a unit used to measure very small areas. It is an area that is the same as that of a 1 mm square. A square millimetre can be written as mm².

100 mm² = 1 cm²

A 1 cm square has an area of 100 mm².

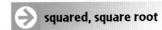 **area, square centimetre, square metre**

square number

A square number is the product of two identical whole numbers.

 squared, square root

$$1 \times 1 = 1 \qquad 2 \times 2 = 4 \qquad 3 \times 3 = 9 \qquad 4 \times 4 = 16 \qquad 5 \times 5 = 25$$

1, 4, 9, 16, 25, ...
These are square numbers.

square root √

A square root of a number is that number which, multiplied by itself, gives that number.

The square root **of 9 is 3**
because $3 \times 3 = 9$.

$$\sqrt{9} = 3$$

→ **square number**

standard unit

Standard units of measurements are units that are agreed by everyone. Metric units and imperial units are both sets of standard units.

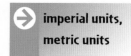 imperial units, metric units

centimetre, metre, kilometre, inch, foot, mile
These are some standard units of length.

gram, kilogram, ounce, pound
These are some standard units of mass.

millilitre, litre, pint, gallon
These are some standard units of capacity.

star

A star can have four or more points. Extending the sides of a regular polygon will make a star. Stars are also polygons.

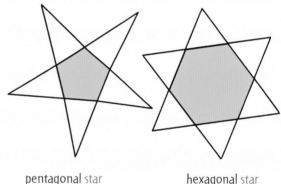

pentagonal star   hexagonal star

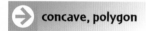 concave, polygon

step

A step is the distance between two points or two numbers. When you walk, your step is the distance between your feet when you walk normally.

 pace, stride

2, 5, 8, 11, 14

This number pattern goes up in steps of 3.

a step

stone

A stone is an imperial unit used to measure weight or mass. A stone weighs about 6 kilograms. Stones used to be the unit used to weigh people.

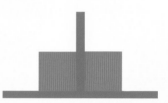

$1 \text{ stone} = 14 \text{ pounds}$

$1 \text{ stone} = 14 \text{ lb}$

$1 \text{ stone} = 6.35 \text{ kg}$

 ounce, pound

straight angle

A straight angle is half a turn. It is two right angles.

 angle, degree, right angle

A straight angle measures 180°.

stride

A stride is the distance from heel to toes when you take a large step.

pace, step

a stride

subset

A subset is part of a larger set. Equilateral triangles is a subset of the set of triangles. A set can have more than one subset.

 attribute, property, set

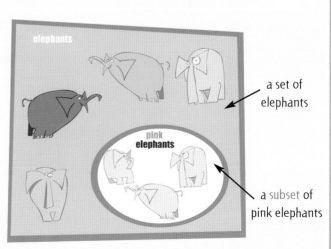

a set of elephants

a subset of pink elephants

subtraction −

subtract
1. Subtraction is taking away one number from another.
2. Subtraction is the difference between two numbers.
3. Subtraction is the inverse of addition.
The sign for subtraction is −.
This is called the minus sign.

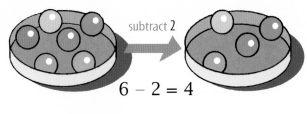

subtract 2

6 − 2 = 4

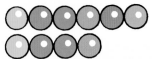

The difference is 6 − 4.

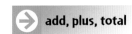

difference, minus, operation,

sum

1. The sum is the result of adding two or more numbers.
2. To sum a set of numbers you must add them.
3. The word sum is often used to mean calculate using addition, subtraction, multiplication, or division. Strictly speaking this is wrong.

add, plus, total

12 + 18
The sum **is** 30.

Sum 11, 15 **and** 20.
Answer 46.

surface

A surface is the face of a shape. It has length and breadth but no thickness.
A surface can be flat or curved.

 face

A cylinder has two flat surfaces and one curved surface.

symbol

A symbol is a sign used to stand for words. It is a mathematical shorthand way of writing something.

 sign

CCVI π ÷ < ≈ % ˚C
These are symbols.

symmetry

symmetrical

There are different types of symmetry. Plane shapes can be symmetrical about a line or have rotational symmetry about a point. Solid shapes can have symmetry about a plane or axis.

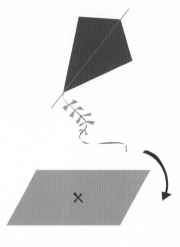

The kite has symmetry about a line.

The parallelogram has rotational symmetry about a point.

The cuboid has symmetry about a plane.

The pyramid has rotational symmetry about an axis.

→ **line of symmetry, rotational symmetry**

Tt

table

When information is written in a list it is often called a table. Multiplication facts written in order are called the multiplication tables. Tables often have rows and columns of information.

→ **chart**

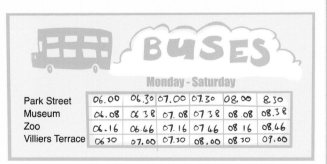

Park Street	06.00	06.30	07.00	07.30	08.00	8.30
Museum	06.08	06.38	07.08	07.38	08.08	08.38
Zoo	06.16	06.46	07.16	07.46	08.16	08.46
Villiers Terrace	06.30	07.00	07.30	08.00	08.30	09.00

a timetable

tally

A tally is a mark which shows how often something happens.

 chart

tally counting

tessellation

Tessellation is a tiling pattern. When you tessellate, you fit shapes together without leaving any gaps between the shapes. Triangles and quadrilaterals will always tessellate.

 pattern

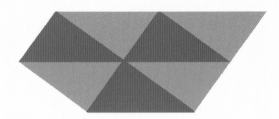

A tessellation of triangles.

tetrahedron

plural *tetrahedra*
A tetrahedron is a solid shape with four sides. Each side will be a triangle. The regular tetrahedron has faces that are equilateral triangles.

 polyhedron, pyramid

a regular tetrahedron

three-dimensional 3D

Three-dimensional shapes are solid shapes. They have length, width, and height. The symbol 3D is short for three-dimensional.

 polyhedron, solid

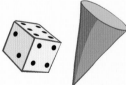

three-dimensional shapes

time

Time is how long something lasts. It is measured in units such as seconds, minutes, hours, days, weeks, months, and years. Clocks and watches are used to tell the time. Stopwatches and timers are used to measure time.

 a.m., p.m., timer

A second is a short time.

A century is a long time.

In one hour's time it will be 4:30.

timer

A timer is an instrument used to measure time. Sand timers, stopwatches, pendulums, clocks, and watches are all different types of timer.

 time

These are timers.

times

Times is how often an addition is to be done.

$$4 \text{ times } 5 = 5 + 5 + 5 + 5$$

 **multiplication**

title

A title tells you the name of something or what something is about. A title is a type of label.

 label

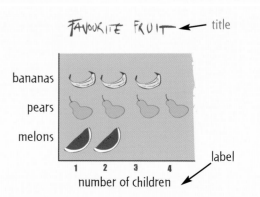

FAVOURITE FRUIT ← title

bananas
pears
melons

1 2 3 4
number of children

label

ton

A ton is an imperial unit used to measure mass or weight. It is a very heavy weight weighing about 1000 kg.

$$1 \, \text{ton} = 2240 \, \text{pounds}$$
$$1 \, \text{ton} = 2240 \, \text{lb}$$
$$1 \, \text{ton} \approx 1016 \, \text{kg}$$

 imperial units , metric ton, tonne

tonne

A tonne is an metric unit used to measure mass or weight. A tonne equals 1000 kilograms. A tonne is sometimes called a metric ton.

$$1 \, \text{tonne} = 1000 \, \text{kilograms}$$
$$1 \, \text{tonne} = 1000 \, \text{kg}$$

 kilogram, metric units, ton

top-heavy fraction

A top-heavy fraction has the numerator larger than the denominator. It is an improper fraction. All top-heavy fractions are greater than 1.

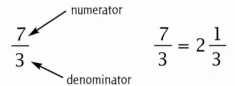

numerator

$$\frac{7}{3}$$

denominator

$$\frac{7}{3} = 2\frac{1}{3}$$

All top-heavy fractions **can be changed to mixed numbers.**

 denominator, improper fraction, mixed number, numerator

total

A total is found by adding all the numbers together. A total is the sum of numbers.

Total 12, 14, and 20 means

$$12 + 14 + 20.$$

The total of 12, 14, and 20 is 46.

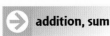 addition, sum

translate

translation

If you translate a shape you slide it to a different position. In a translation you do not turn or rotate the shape.

 reflect, rotate, slide

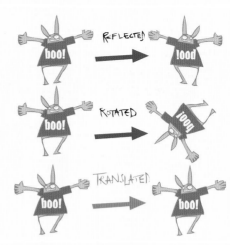

trapezium

plural *trapezia*

A trapezium is a 4-sided shape that has one pair of sides that are parallel. The other two sides are not parallel.

trapezium   right-angled   isosceles
               trapezium   trapezium

 parallel, quadrilateral

treble

If you treble something, you multiply it by three.

 double

Treble **6** is **18.**

10 *trebled* is **30.**

tree diagram

A tree diagram can be used for sorting. When using a tree diagram you often have to make a YES or NO choice.

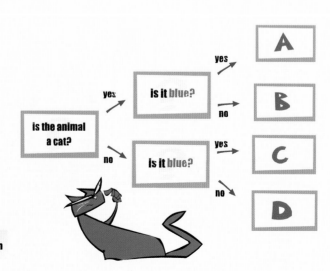

In this tree diagram the cat would be sorted into box A.

 Carroll diagram, Venn diagram

triangle

triangular

A triangle is any polygon that has three sides. The three angles of a triangle add up to 180°. All triangles will tessellate. The words equilateral, isosceles, and scalene tell you about the sides of a triangle. The words acute, obtuse, and right-angled tell you about the angles of a triangle. A triangular shape has three sides.

Triangles have 3 sides and 3 angles.

→ **acute, equilateral, isosceles, obtuse, polygon, right-angled, scalene**

triangle numbers

Triangle numbers are 1, 3, 6, 10, 15, 21, …. The difference between neighbouring triangle numbers increases by 1 each time.

→ **prime numbers, square numbers**

Triangle numbers make a triangle pattern.

triangular prism

A triangular prism is a prism that has triangular ends. The end can be any type of triangle.

→ **polyhedron, prism, solid**

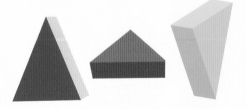

A triangular prism has five faces.

triangular pyramid

A triangular pyramid is a pyramid with a triangle base. It is another name for a tetrahedron.

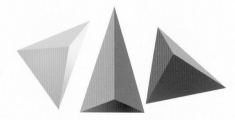

→ **polyhedron, pyramid, tetrahedron**

Each face of the four faces of a triangular pyramid is a triangle.

triple

Triple is a set of three
or three times as much.

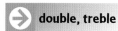
→ double, treble

Triple 5 is 15.
The triple (3, 4, 12) can be written:

$$3 \times 4 = 12, \ 4 \times 3 = 12;$$
$$12 \div 4 = 3, \ 12 \div 3 = 4.$$

turn

When something turns it spins,
rotates, revolves, or whirls.

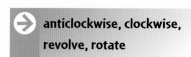
→ anticlockwise, clockwise,
revolve, rotate

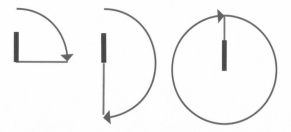

A quarter, a half, and a full turn in a clockwise direction.

two-dimensional 2D

Two-dimensional shapes
are flat shapes. They have
length and width but no
thickness.
The symbol 2D is short
for two-dimensional.

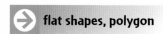
→ flat shapes, polygon

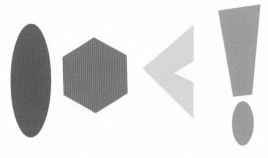

two-dimensional shapes

Uu

unequal ≠

If two things are unequal they are not equal.
The sign for unequal is ≠.

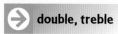
→ double, treble

$$3 \times 8 \neq 25$$
$$3 \times 8 = 24$$

unit

1. Unit is a name for 'one'.
Hundreds, tens, and units are
used in place value.
2. Units are used in measuring.
Metres are units used to
measure length.

 1. **place value**

2. **imperial units, metric units,
standard units**

tens
hundreds ↓ units
↘ 173 ↙

Litre is a unit of capacity.

Kilogram is a unit of mass.

Kilometre is a unit of distance.

V

The Romans used the letter V to
stand for the number 5.

 Roman numerals

I V X L C D M
Roman numerals

$V = 5$
$VI = 6$
$VII = 7$

value

The value of something is what
it is worth.

 place value

tens
hundreds ↓ units
↘ 173 ↙

The value of the digit 7 is 70.

The value of $(7 + 3) \times 4$ is 40.

Venn diagram

A Venn diagram is used for
sorting sets of things.

A Venn diagram used to sort some shapes.

 Carroll diagram, tree diagram

shapes

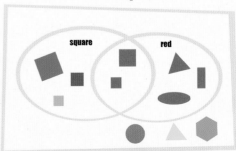

vertex

plural *vertices*

A vertex is the corner of a plane or solid shape. Vertices are where sides or straight edges meet.

→ **edge, face**

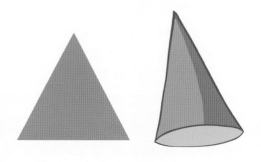

A triangle has 3 vertices.   A cone has 1 vertex.

vertical

A vertical line is at right angles to a horizontal line. A vertical line goes up and down.

→ **perpendicular**

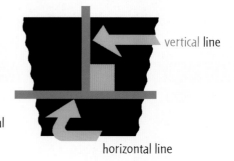

Vertical and horizontal lines meet at 90°.

vertical line

horizontal line

volume

Volume is the amount of space taken up by a solid shape. When measuring volume, cubic units such as cm³ and m³ are used.

→ **cubic centimetre, cubic metre**

A 1 cm cube has a volume of $1 \times 1 \times 1$ cm³ = 1 cm³.

A 2 cm cube has a volume of $2 \times 2 \times 2$ cm³ = 8 cm³.

vote

If you vote, you are given a choice and you choose which you want. The thing with most votes is the favourite.

→ **tally**

spot party

wig party

stripe party

Most people voted for the wig party.

vulgar fraction

A vulgar fraction is an ordinary fraction that has a numerator smaller than a denominator.

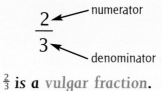

$$\frac{2}{3}$$ is a vulgar fraction.

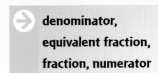 denominator, equivalent fraction, fraction, numerator

weigh

You weigh to find out how heavy something is. To weigh something you use a balance or scales.

mass, weight

You can weigh yourself using scales.

weight

weights

Weight is the heaviness of something. Weight is the force with which an object is pulled towards the centre of the Earth. The word 'weight' is often used instead of 'mass' even though they are not quite the same.

100 kg

mass

Units of mass are called weights.

whole number

Whole numbers are the numbers you use to count with. Whole numbers are the positive integers including zero. A fraction is not a whole number.

$$0, 1, 2, 3, 4, 5, \ldots$$

Whole numbers **go on to infinity.**

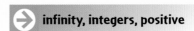 infinity, integers, positive

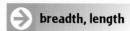

width

The width is the distance from one side to the other and is sometimes called the breadth. When measuring length and width, the width is usually the shorter length.

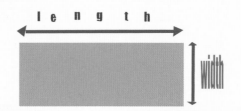

length

width

→ breadth, length

X

The Romans used the letter X to stand for the number 10.

I V X L C D M
Roman numerals

$X = 10$
$XI = 11$
$XV = 15$
$XXX = 30$

→ Roman numerals

---

x

The sign for multiplication is ×. The sign × means 'multiplied by'.

$3 \times 5 = 15$

Three multiplied by 5 equals fifteen.

→ multiply

---

x-axis

The horizontal axis of a graph is sometimes called the x-axis. The vertical axis is called the y-axis.

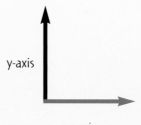

y-axis

x-axis

→ axis, coordinates

---

x-coordinate

The x-coordinate is the horizontal distance from the origin. It is the first number in the number pair.

(4,6)

The x-coordinate is 4.

The y-coordinate is 6.

→ axis, coordinates

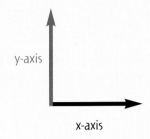

y-axis

The vertical axis of a graph is sometimes called the y-axis. The horizontal axis is called the x-axis.

y-axis

x-axis

→ axis, coordinates

y-coordinate

The y-coordinate is the vertical distance from the origin. It is the second number in the number pair.

(4,6)

The x-coordinate is 4.

The y-coordinate is 6.

→ axis, coordinates

yard

A yard is an imperial unit used to measure distance. There are three feet in one yard. A yard is about 90 cm.

$1 \ yard = 3 \ feet$

$1 \ yard = 36 \ inches$

$1 \ yard = 91.44 \ cm$

→ foot, imperial units, inches

year

A year is how long it takes the Earth to make a revolution around the Sun. It takes just over 365 days for the Earth to travel round the Sun. Every fourth year is a leap year.

$1 \ year = 365 \ days$

$1 \ leap \ year = 366 \ days$

$1 \ year = 12 \ months$

→ AD, BC, calendar, leap year, month

Zz

zero 0

Zero is another word for nothing or nought. Zeros are used as a place holder in large numbers. Zero is an integer that separates positive and negative numbers. The sign for zero is 0.

$$5 - 5 = 0 \qquad 5 \times 0 = 0$$

$$5 \quad 50 \quad 500 \quad 5000$$

The zeros change the value of the digit 5

Zero separates positive and negative numbers.

 integer, place value

Apparatus

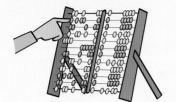

abacus

digit cards

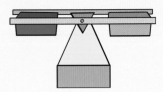

balance

calculator

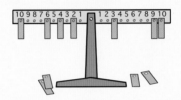

equalizer

dice

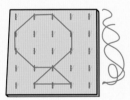

geoboard

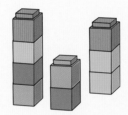

interlocking cubes

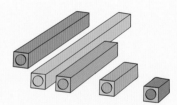

number rods

measuring jug

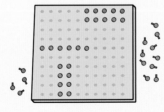

pegboard

number cards

number fan

sand timer

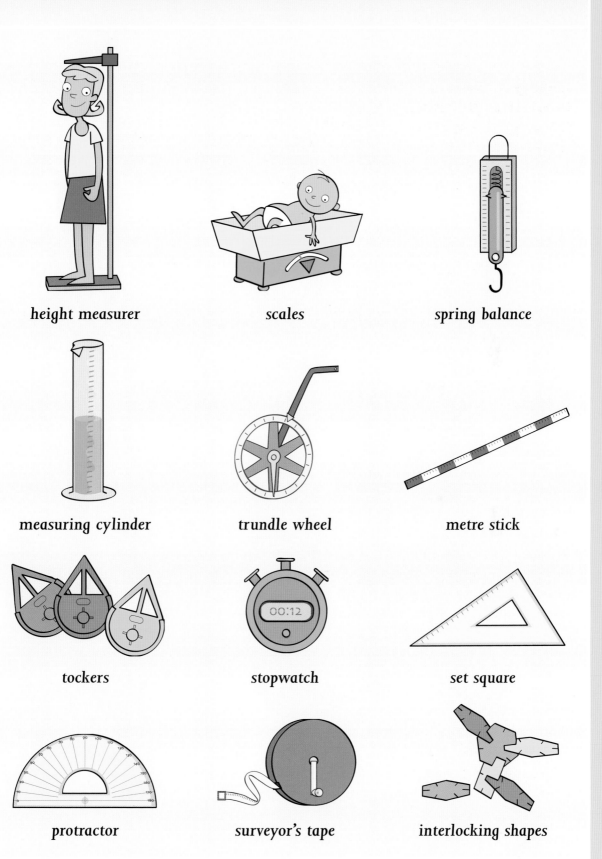

height measurer

scales

spring balance

measuring cylinder

trundle wheel

metre stick

tockers

stopwatch

set square

protractor

surveyor's tape

interlocking shapes

Months of the year

January *31 days*
Named after the Roman god Janus

February *28 days* (29 in a leap year)
Named after a Roman festival called Frebrualia

March *31 days*
Named after the Roman god Mars

April *30 days*
Named after the Greek goddess Aphrodite

May *31 days*
Named after the Greek goddess Maia

June *30 days*
Named after the Roman goddess Juno

July *31 days*
Named after Julius Caesar

August *31 days*
Named after Augustus Caesar

September *30 days*
Was once the seventh month of the year

October *31 days*
Was once the eighth month of the year

November *30 days*
Was once the ninth month of the year

December *31 days*
Was once the tenth month of the year

The year used to start with the month of March. This made September, October, November, and December the 7th, 8th, 9th, and 10th months. Julius Caesar changed the start of the year from March to January in the year 45BC.

Days of the week

Sunday is named after the sun.
Monday is named after the moon.
Tuesday is named after the Norse god called Tiw.
Wednesday is named after the Norse god called Woden.
Thursday is named after the Norse god called Thor.
Friday is named after the Norse god called Frigg.
Saturday is named after the Roman god called Saturn.

Instruction words

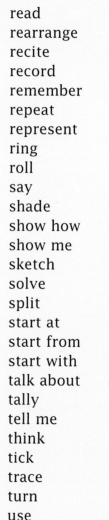

answer
arrange
bisect
build
calculate
carry on
change
change over
chant
check
choose
clear
collect
colour
compare
complete
construct
continue
convert
copy
cost
count
count back
count on
count to
cross
decide
define
describe
discuss
draw
end

estimate
exchange
explain
fill in
find
finish
fold
how many?
identify
imagine
interpret
investigate
join
join in
join up
justify
listen
look at
make
match
method
name
order
pick out
place
plot
point to
predict
present
prove
put
question

read
rearrange
recite
record
remember
repeat
represent
ring
roll
say
shade
show how
show me
sketch
solve
split
start at
start from
start with
talk about
tally
tell me
think
tick
trace
turn
use
work out
write

121

Position and direction words

above
across
after
along
anticlockwise
apart
around
away
backward
bearing
before
behind
below
beside
between
bottom
clockwise
close to
column
coordinate
diagonal
direction

down
east
edge
forward
from
half-way
horizontal
in
in front
inside
intersection
left
middle
near
next to
north

north-east
north-west
oblique
off
on
opposite
origin
outside
over
parallel
pendicular
right
route
row
side

south
south-east
south-west
through
to
top
towards
under
underneath
up
vertical
west

Chance words

biased
certain
certainty
chance
definitely
doubtful
equal chance
equally likely

even chance
evens
fair
fifty-fifty chance
impossible
least common
least popular
likely

likelihood
maybe
most common
most popular
odds
possible
possibility
probable

probability
random
rare
uncertain
unfair
unlikely

Money words

amount	dear, dearer, dearest	note
bought	discount	pay
buy	expensive	price
change	gain	profit
cheap, cheaper, cheapest	interest	sale
coin	interest rate	sell
cost	least expensive	selling price
cost price	loss	sold
costs less	money	spend
costs more	most expensive	spent

Mathematical symbols

+	plus, add, positive	≤	is less than or equal to	m	metre
−	minus, subtract, negative	≥	is greater than or equal to	km	kilometre
×	multiplied by			ml	millilitre
÷	divided by	%	percentage	dl	decilitre
√	square root	∞	infinity	cl	centilitre
$\sqrt[3]{}$	cube root		parallel	l	litre
^{0}	degree			r	remainder
=	equals		perpendicular	^{0}C	degrees Celcius
≠	does not equal	g	gram	^{0}F	degrees Fahrenheit
≈	is approximately equal to	kg	kilogram	mm^2	square millimetres
		mm	millimetre	cm^2	square centimetres
<	is less than	cm	centimetre	m^2	square metres
>	is greater than	dm	decimetre	km^2	square kilometres
				π	pi, 3.142, $\frac{22}{7}$

Useful mathematical tables

Length

10 millimetres (mm) = 1 centimetre (cm)
10 centimetres (cm) = 1 decimetre (dm)
10 decimetres (dm) = 1 metre (m)
1000metres (m) = 1 kilometre (km)

Weight, mass

1000 grams (g) = 1 kilogram (kg)
1000 kilograms (kg) = 1 tonne (t)

Capacity

10 millilitres (ml) = 1 centilitre (cl)
10 centilitres (cl) = 1 decilitre (dl)
10 decilitres (dl) = 1 litre (l)

Time

60 seconds (sec) = 1 minute (min)
60 minutes (min) = 1 hour (h)
24 hours (h) = 1 day
7 days = 1 week
52 weeks = 1 year
365 days = 1 year
366 days = 1 leap year
12 months = 1 year
10 years = 1 decade
100 years= 1 century
1000 years = 1 millennium

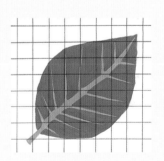

Volume

1000 cubic millimetres (mm^3) = 1 cubic centimetre (cm^3)
1000 cubic centimetres (cm^3) = 1 cubic decimetre (dm^3)
1000 cubic decimetres (dm^3) = 1 cubic metre (m^3)

Area

100 square millimetres (mm^2) = 1 square centimetre (cm^2)
100 square centimetres (cm^2) = 1 square decimetre (dm^2)
100 square decimetres (dm^2) = 1 square metre (m^2)
1 000 000 square metres (m^2) = 1 square kilometre (km^2)

Useful mathematical formulae

Area of a rectangle = length × breadth
Area = L × B

Perimeter of a rectangle is 2 × (length + breadth)
Perimeter = 2 × (L+B)

Area of a circle = π × radius squared
Area= π × r^2

Circumference of a circle = π × diameter
Circumference= π × D

Index